HOW TO BABY-PROOF YOUR HOME

To Mary Frances,

You've been a terrific
Health Visitor. Thanks for
all your help.

With love

Lisa x

HOW TO
BABY-PROOF
YOUR HOME

LISA BROWNLIE

MAINSTREAM
PUBLISHING

EDINBURGH AND LONDON

The medical advice given in this book is for guidance only. It is highly recommended that before attempting any of the life-saving techniques described in this book you should first of all be confident of your abilities through having undertaken a training course, such as those provided by the ambulance service. The author and the publishers cannot accept responsibility for any injury or damage suffered as a result of undertaking any medical techniques in this book.

First published in Great Britain in 1998 by
MAINSTREAM PUBLISHING COMPANY (EDINBURGH) LTD
7 Albany Street
Edinburgh EH1 3UG

ISBN 1 85158 934 1

A catalogue record for this book is available from the British Library

Typeset in 11 on 13pt Sabon
Printed and bound in Finland by WSOY

To my boys Michael and Andrew; my nephews and nieces Andrew, Emma, Kirsten, Matthew, Kayleigh and Rhyss; my husband John and to my mother Joyce Brownlie. Thanks for always being there JB.

CONTENTS

CHAPTER ONE

SHOULD I BABY-PROOF MY HOME?

Every responsible parent should take steps to keep their child safe from harm. How far you actually go in baby-proofing your home is up to you.

How To Baby-proof Your Home has been written to raise attention to the many ways in which your child could hurt himself. It is by no means complete – as no book could ever completely cover every risk your child will face as he goes through life – but it will, hopefully, highlight the causes of many household accidents and will allow parents to take preventative measures to minimise the chance of an accident happening.

Remember that baby-proofing is not just for your child's sake, but for yours too. It is an opportunity for you to remove valuable and sentimental items that, if something happened to them you would be upset about. But do not confuse baby-proofing with turning your home into a soulless place devoid of possessions and character.

Simply by clearing out your kitchen's floor-level cupboards of sharp or heavy items, or installing cupboard locks or electrical socket covers means that you are baby-proofing your home.

Many families baby-proof their bedrooms just by putting their mattress on the floor and packing away the frame so that a baby will not get hurt if he crawls off the bed.

If you are serious about making sure your home is as safe for your child as can be reasonably expected then you must begin by examining it from his height.

Looking at your home from your child's perspective is always the first step: get down on your hands and knees and crawl about searching for things that he might see.

Get in to the habit of using safety gates and cupboard locks before your child is born. This will give your family time to get into the habit of closing and locking doors and putting things away.

Remember that all children are different. Your first child might never have played on the stairs or opened an outside door. Your second, third or fourth child will have his own personality and will do things differently from his brothers and sisters.

It's a sad fact of life that accidents are the biggest killers of children, with the majority of these accidents happening in and around the home. In 1995, more than two million children went to Accident and Emergency departments as a result of their injuries – almost half of these were as a result of an accident in the home. Tragically 504 children aged 14 years and under died that same year from accidents.

As your baby grows, teach him to become more and more safety conscious. Devise your own 'Safety Vocabulary' right from the start using simple words like:

'No', 'Hot', 'Don't touch', 'Ouch', 'Hurt' and 'Burny, burny'.

As your baby grows into a toddler you can begin to explain more clearly that fires are hot; that medicines are not sweeties and that knives are sharp. Use your vocabularly often and explain to your toddler at every opportunity why he should not do certain things. Little by little your toddler will learn some sense of safety and you will be achieving what every responsible and loving parent should.

Many accidents happen to children because they do not concentrate, with some children appearing to be more accident-prone than others. Statistics show that boys suffer far more accidents than girls. In 1995, 347 boys and 157 girls aged 14 years and under died as a result of an accident.

It's not known whether this is just the way boys are or that in some way we encourage them with the old adage 'boys will be boys'.

As children grow the types of accidents they will be vulnerable to will change. A vigilant parent will be aware of this and will seek ways to help safeguard their child as he develops.

From the time an infant starts to wriggle he will be vulnerable to accidents. For example, if he is left alone on a changing table, he could roll off onto the floor below.

When a baby starts to pull himself up and crawl, he is opening up the vista of accident opportunities, such as falling down stairs or toppling over a heavy item as he pulls himself up on it.

A child's first steps are seen by parents as a major milestone in his development, something to be applauded. But it is also a major opportunity for many more accidents, some of them serious. A child is no sooner walking than it is running and climbing. Once again, it is time to re-evaluate your home for potential accident spots.

Once a parent gets to know their child's personality they can usually predict whether they're in for a lifetime of bumps and bruises or not. It is also important that parents realise the extent to which a child can understand things.

While an infant cannot comprehend what you are saying, by the time that child reaches his first birthday it is reasonable to expect him to understand what 'yes' and 'no' mean.

Until a child is about three years old they will probably repeat similar accidents. For example, your toddler might hurt his fingers by closing a door on them and although it was a painful experience he won't remember not to do it again.

While it's never too soon to start teaching children basic safety, it's not until a child is about three years old that he will begin to understand the consequences of certain actions.

CHAPTER TWO

THE KITCHEN

The kitchen is the most dangerous place in your house for small children. Hazards are hard to spot in a cluttered kitchen, which is why it's vital that the kitchen area is regularly cleaned and all appliances and kitchen items are safely put away.

Prevent slips by wiping up any spills immediately, and keep *all* play activities out of the kitchen.

Keep baby-bouncers off worktops and tables.

If you have a telephone in the kitchen, do not use long cords that a child could trip over or wrap around their necks. Cordless phones are ideal for keeping an eye on a wandering child while making an important call.

Dangling appliance cords provide another opportunity for your little explorer. He may give it a little tug or swing it backwards and forwards. Your child could not only bring the appliance, such as a recently boiled kettle or hot iron, down on to his head, but also anything else in its path such as a sharp knife, an opened bottle of cleaning fluid, a cup of hot tea or a glass that could shatter all over the floor.

The same potential disasters could happen if your child tugs on a table cloth only to find the entire contents of the family's evening meal, including crockery, lands on his head.

POISONS

Detergents, bleach, oven cleaners, furniture polish and other lethal mixtures must be kept in a locked cupboard away from all food and preferably not under the sink even if it has a safety-catch. These cleaners are too dangerous to risk putting in your child's reach and your child may be too determined to be deterred by a safety-catch. Approximately 30,000 children a year attend an Accident and Emergency department suffering from poisoning or suspected poisoning. Once you have removed all cleaners, give the bottom of the cupboard a wash. Children can, and have, been poisoned by the chemical residue. Only buy cleaning products and other hazardous chemicals in child-resistant containers. You should also see if you can buy Bitrex-protected cleaning agents. Many manufacturers include a substance called Bitrex in their products; it tastes disgusting and makes the child spit out whichever noxious substance it had been intent on drinking.

Keep all rodent and insect poisons in a locked cupboard or on a high shelf well out of children's reach in a locked garage or shed. And always store dangerous household chemicals in their own containers. Never decant them into old food or drink containers.

While using a poisonous substance, such as bleach, do not leave it lying out unattended. If you go to answer the telephone or door, put it away or take it with you. Remember, most accidents, including poisonings, happen within moments – leave nothing to chance.

BURNS

A young child does not understand that some of his actions could hurt him; nor does he know how to get himself out of a dangerous situation. A child who crawls into a puddle of boiling water, will stay put and scream. He will rarely try and get out of the path of what is hurting him.

Scald-burns are the most common type of burn among young children. The majority of scalds are caused by hot foods and drinks, hot tap water and food or drinks prepared in a microwave.

Children, particularly those aged six months to two years old, are commonly burned from hot foods and liquids spilled in the kitchen, or where food is served. A cup of hot tea or coffee is an attraction to a young child as they see their parent drink it and believe it is something that they will enjoy too.

Sally's mum, Jane, was in the kitchen making herself a morning cup of coffee when the telephone started to ring. The eight-month-old baby was happily crawling around the floor when Jane dashed off to answer it, taking the steaming mug with her. It was Jane's mum. They spoke for only a few minutes when their conversation was cut short by Sally's screams.

She rushed into the kitchen to find her daughter lying on the floor next to a puddle of scalding water. Jane grabbed the child from the floor and immediately saw the red welts rising on her skin. Jane rushed Sally into the bathroom and started dosing her child with ice-cold water in the bath.

The burns looked very serious, so Jane dialled 999 and frantically explained what had happened. An ambulance was dispatched and took Jane, Sally and her older son, three-year-old Simon, who was also in the kitchen but who was unharmed, to hospital where doctors treated the severe burns to Sally's neck, hands and feet.

It later transpired that while Jane was on the telephone, Simon had pulled on the kettle's long cord and sent the kettle toppling onto the floor spraying freshly boiled water all over it. Baby Sally then crawled through it.

Sally's had to endure years of skin grafts to the affected areas and today still bears a reminder of how easily accidents can happen.

COOKER

Children and cookers are a potential recipe for disaster. Mealtime preparation is such a real danger zone that young children should not be allowed in the kitchen. Of course, this is not always possible, especially if it means leaving a child unattended in a separate room. So, if a child must be in the kitchen, make sure you have some rules about behaviour or put your youngster in his high-chair or play-pen.

Teach your child that the oven is not for touching. As mentioned earlier, employ your 'danger vocabulary'. Repeat at every opportunity that the oven is 'hot' perhaps adding the phrase: 'No touch! Hot! Hot! No touch!'

Pots of hot food or boiling water frequently leave children with severe burns when they are accidentally knocked off the cooker or a child has pulled one on to himself. When cooking, try to use the back burners only and keep all pot handles turned away from the cooker's edge. Remember to be careful not to heat up the handle over another burner. For extra protection, invest in a cooker guard.

Check all pots and pans for loose handles and tighten if need be. If the handles will not tighten, throw them away.

If you have a gas cooker, regularly check the pilot lights to ensure it is in good working order. Carbon monoxide, which is present in gas, is a silent killer.

Your cooker is not an alternative heating system for your home, do not use it as such.

Ovens are often at an ideal height to burn toddlers and crawling babies. They should never be used without an oven guard or while your child is in the room.

Never store your child's cereals and snacks above the cooker, as this will encourage climbing expeditions. Move them to a cupboard as far away from the cooker as possible and preferably a low shelf to prevent your child from climbing on to worktops or the cooker.

Do not hang curtains or tea towels too close to the cooker. Nor should you leave pot-holders, food wrappings and recipes near the burners

Install a smoke-detector and a fire extinguisher in your kitchen and check them regularly. Keep the fire extinguisher out of reach of small children, and teach older children how to use it properly. Warn them not to try to fight a fire if it gets too big; they must know when to get out of the house.

Long, loose sleeves should not be worn while cooking – they could catch on a pot handle and spill its contents on to the floor and your child or they could catch fire.

Clean the cooker and grill regularly to keep it free

from grease and food. If you use aluminium foil in the grill pan change it after each use.

Children love to play with dials, knobs or buttons – often with disastrous effects. Take the knobs off all appliances until it is time to cook or switch your cooker off at the mains. If your oven is powered by gas, it might be useful to keep it turned off at the tap, if it's accessible, until you need it. A child playing with gas can easily start a fire or cause an explosion.

Chip-pan fires – never throw water on a chip-pan fire. Cover the pan with a damp dish-cloth or tea towel.

Do not let your child play by your feet while cooking – not only could you trip over him you could also spill boiling hot food or fat onto your child.

Never leave a boiling pot or sizzling frying-pan unattended on the cooker.

MICROWAVE

Never let a child use a microwave until he or she is old enough to read and understand how it works. Take the time to review the handbook's instructions and safe-operating procedures. Stress the importance of always reading and following the directions printed on the packet, especially cooling, stirring and standing times. Even when your child appears proficient at using the microwave, ask him to double-check with you on power-settings and times before heating any new foods. Warn your child that metal and microwaves do not mix and could start a fire.

Tell your child that the containers that are used to cook the food will be hot and to make sure that he always uses pot holders before removing anything from the oven.

If your appliance does not have a child safety-lock, and your child enjoys pushing the buttons on appliances, it might be an idea to keep a mug of water inside the microwave in case he touches the start button. Otherwise switch it off at the mains. Also make sure the seal of your microwave door is not cracked or caked with food which, although slight, could cause a danger of radiation.

Make sure your child understands that the microwave cooks food from the inside out. So while food may feel cool on the outside, it could be very hot in the middle. Teach him the importance of stirring food both during and after cooking.

It is best not to heat baby foods or milk in the microwave. If you decide to use your microwave for this, use a low power setting and make sure you thoroughly mix the food or milk before giving it to your child. Microwave ovens form hot pockets which could seriously burn your baby's mouth and throat.

Teach your child some cooking tips, such as:
- Always prick foods with tight skins, such as sausages and egg yolks, before putting them into the oven as they can explode after cooking.
- Escaping steam can burn. Always open the bag, pull back the cover or remove plastic wrap away from themselves and others.
- Vent microwave containers properly by piercing cling-film with a fork, by folding back a corner of the plastic wrap, or placing the container's lid loosely on top. Trapped steam could cause an explosion.

DISHWASHERS

Never leave knives or other sharp cooking utensils in the dishwasher or on the worktop. Immediately after use, wash them by hand and put them safely away. By the very nature of dishwashers, the sharp-ends of utensils have to be placed facing upwards in the cutlery basket for proper cleaning. If they are left in the basket in an open dishwasher, a child could fall onto the basket and seriously injure or kill himself. Get into the habit of firmly closing and locking your dishwasher – if it has a locking-mechanism – every time you use it.

Dishwasher doors that are left open can prove an attractive playing place. An unanchored machine may tilt forward causing objects to fall on to your child. Or he may hurt himself on sharp items that have been loaded into the machine.

It had been a long day at the Harold household. Gerard had just celebrated his sixth birthday with an afternoon party at his home. His friends and cousins had just left, tired after a long session of party games, cakes and sweets.

Mum, Janet, was in the kitchen with her sister, clearing away leftover sandwiches, juice and cake. She'd told Gerard and his older brother, Sam, to tidy up the living-room and to take Gerard's new toys up to the bedroom they shared.

But the boys were still over-excited from the day's events. They ran about the living-room kicking the new football Gerard had received as one of his presents.

The ball rolled into the kitchen and Gerard's

mum shouted at him to get the ball and take it upstairs.

Gerard, in his stockinged feet, ran into the kitchen at full speed. As he did, he slipped on the floor and fell head first towards the opened dishwasher his mother was still loading with dishes.

Gerard's head came down inches from the cutlery basket; however, a large knife protruding from the basket slashed open the main jugular artery in his neck.

Gerard died almost instantaneously.

It was an accident which could almost be described as a 'freak' one. Yet the risk of something like this happening is very real. Manufacturers recommend that cutlery be placed handle-side down for efficient cleaning. And due to the design of dishwashers, the cutlery basket is in a very vulnerable position for children as it sits on the bottom tray.

Never allow children in the kitchen when loading or unloading the dishwasher and always lift the cutlery basket out of the machine first when unloading and then load it up in the sink or on a worktop before placing it back into the machine as the very last item. Always ensure the dishwasher door is properly closed and locked if possible to stop children from playing inside it.

Remember to keep dishwasher detergents out of your child's reach. They are extremely dangerous. Children have sampled these cleaning powders from open dishwasher doors or from the box left in an accessible area and suffered severe internal burns and death.

Keep your sink for kitchen duties and never bathe your

child in it while the dishwasher or washing-machine is running. Your baby can be severely burned if hot waste-water backs up through the sink. Many appliances have their own water-heating system which could make the water much hotter than your tap water.

Remember too that dishwasher doors can get extremely hot during use.

APPLIANCES

Refrigerators, chest freezers, washing-machines and tumble driers could prove fatal to children who could easily climb into any one of these appliances. If the door should close on them tight-fitting gaskets will cut off the air supply. And as many appliances are well insulated a child's screams might go unheard.

Warn your child of the dangers of playing inside an appliance.

A game of hide and seek turned to tragedy for one three-year-old child.

Little Jamie loved to play hide-and-seek with his puppy. The two would spend hours chasing each other and romping on the floor.

As usual, after Jamie's mum had left for work and his dad fed his younger brother his breakfast, the toddler went off to play with his pet.

As he was finishing off the feeding, Jamie's dad noticed how quiet the house had become. After a quick look around the house he noticed the bolt was off the gate and thought Jamie had wandered off.

His dad frantically went round the nearby

houses and streets with the help of his neighbours. When there was no sign of him the police were called in to help with the search.

The police co-ordinated their search of the surrounding area as well as inside the family's home. An hour after the toddler disappeared, Jamie was found by the police. He was dead.

Police discovered Jamie inside the tumble-drier with the door closed. Experts later said he probably suffocated within minutes of the door closing.

After the accident, his distraught parents described how fascinated Jamie was with the tumble-drier. How he would stick his head inside the machine and shout and giggle because he liked the sound of his voice inside it.

His parents had never known him to climb inside the machine before and, tragically, police believe he might have climbed in to the machine as part of his hide-and-seek game with his puppy, who may have accidently shut the door as he jumped up at the boy.

The doors of washing machines and tumble-driers can also become very hot. It might be worthwhile keeping your child out of the kitchen or laundry room while these machines are in operation.

FRIDGE/FREEZER

Ice trays or the freezer compartment of the fridge, in particular the small, under-the-worktop ones which are more easily accessible, can prove a painful experience for your youngster if he touches them with wet hands or his tongue as they may stick to them and removing them could mean your child losing a layer of skin.

Anything that resembles food can prove too much of a temptation for young children. If your fridge is adorned with magnets, especially food-shaped ones, remove them and invest in a conventional notice-board placed high up on a wall.

ELECTRIC KITCHEN GADGETS

Kitchen gadgets are a real life-saver for the busy mum. But plugging too many into the same socket could overload your system and cause a blow-out or fire. If you live in an older home it's a good idea to have a qualified electrician check your home's wiring.

If your lights dim or circuit-breakers blow when you use an appliance, consult an electrician. Another warning sign is discoloured outlets.

Do not plug too many appliances into the same socket and reduce your child's risk of a shock by checking that all of your appliances' electrical leads and plugs are in good condition. Replace and repair any that are frayed or worn.

Do not allow children access to electric leads. Children have accidently strangled or electrocuted themselves while playing with them.

Keep appliances, such as toasters, radios or kettles, where your child cannot reach them. A child can be electrocuted if they attempt to plug them in. Keep them away from the sink, too. If one falls in the water, it can give your child a nasty shock or kill him even if you have turned the appliance off.

After every use, unplug and put away all small appliances.

Be on guard for appliances that can get hot, like toasters, and keep them out of reach. Similarly, never leave an iron, either on or off, lying about. A dangling cord is far too much of a temptation. Leave it somewhere safe to cool down after use.

WORKTOPS, CUPBOARDS AND DRAWERS

Never sit your child on the worktop. Besides the danger of a fall, they can easily reach for items that can harm them.

Use safety-catches to keep cupboards and drawers off-limits to your child.

Set aside at least one cupboard for your child to explore and play with. Store safe items such as Tupperware, small cereal boxes and lightweight, non-breakable pots and pans.

Keep bin-bags and plastic wrap in a drawer or cabinet with a safety-catch.

Keep aluminium foil and cling-film boxes out of children's reach. The serrated edges can easily cut little fingers.

BIN-BAGS, CARRIER BAGS, AND OTHER PLASTIC WRAPS

Children have suffocated when plastic bags, usually bin-bags, carrier bags or dry-cleaning bags, have blocked their noses and mouths and prevented them from breathing. A child does not have to pull a bag over its head to suffocate. Keep all plastic bags away from children and never use them as a mattress cover.

Mealtimes

A child who does not have all of his teeth is at risk of choking as he may try to swallow food whole. The risk is further complicated by the fact that a young child's reflex to cough that food back up is not yet fully developed.

Cut food into small pieces. If your child crams large amounts of food into his mouth at once, limit the size of portions you give him. As your child grows older you should maintain a careful eye while he eats to make sure he chews his food well.

Finger-foods like popcorn, grapes and sausage chunks are a common cause of choking. Do not give these foods to your baby.

Young children should not be given breakable plates, bowls or cups.

Your child should always be seated when eating. A running toddler with a mouthful of food risks choking.

And while this piece of advice may be good manners, it's also good practice – never talk with your mouth full and never allow your child to eat while lying down.

Ban table-cloths from use until your children are older. It's very easy for a tug on the cloth to bring down a hot drink or an entire meal onto a child's head. Use place mats instead.

Do not leave pet bowls on the floor after your pet has finished its meals. Young children have been known to choke to death on pet food and small babies can drown in pets' water bowls. Remember a child can drown in an inch of water.

High-chairs

Never seat your baby in a high-chair without using

proper seat restraints. A tray is not enough to keep a child in the chair.

Make sure the high-chair's legs are stable when setting it up and position it away from walls, tables or worktops where the child may be able to tip the chair over.

Your child should not be permitted to climb into the chair by himself nor should older children be allowed to use it as a climbing-frame, especially when a baby is in it.

Keep the chair clean and in good working order. Replace any broken or worn parts immediately.

BOOSTERS AND TRAVEL HIGH-CHAIRS

Ensure booster seats or travel high-chairs are strapped firmly to a chair with no slippage in accordance with the manufacturer's instructions.

As with high-chairs, always use the seat's restraints and make sure your child cannot tip over by pushing himself off another chair or other objects with his feet.

Never prop your child up at the table on cushions. These can be quite unstable and can result in a nasty fall.

RUBBISH

Your bin is a veritable playground to a child who enjoys a good rummage in search of interesting playthings, or even food. Keep your bin in a locked cupboard.

When disposing of broken glass, always double-wrap it before placing in the bin.

Always tie knots in plastic bags before throwing them away to prevent a child suffocating himself with one.

PESTICIDES

Since we do not fully understand the effects of pesticides,

protect your family by carefully washing all fruit and vegetables with water and a scrubbing-brush. Throw away the outside leaves of other leafy vegetables. Peeling may reduce the amount of pesticide residue and the Government currently recommends that parents should only give *peeled* apples and carrots to children. Alternatively you could buy organic produce.

CHECKLIST

Below is a kitchen-safety checklist for easy reference. Obviously, the more safety tips you employ in your home the safer a place it will be for your child.

❑ Store all hazardous chemicals in their own child resistant containers.

❑ Move poisonous chemicals to a locked cupboard and out of children's reach. Do not store them under the sink. After moving chemicals, wash any residue from the bottom of the cupboard.

❑ Ensure curtains, food wrappers and recipes are not near the cooker's burners when in use.

❑ Keep children's cereals and snacks in a cupboard away from the cooker.

❑ Install a smoke-detector just outside your kitchen door.

❑ Buy a fire extinguisher and teach older children how to use it.

❑ If possible, remove cooker knobs or make sure you switch the cooker off at the mains when not in use.

❑ Buy a cooker guard for the front of the cooker and an oven guard for the front of your oven.

❑ Check all pots and pans. Either repair or throw away damaged items.

❑ Teach older children how to cook safely with the microwave.

❑ Make sure your microwave's door seal is in good condition.

❑ Teach your child the dangers of hiding in dishwashers, washing-machines and refrigerators.

❑ Never leave dishwasher detergents in your child's reach.

❑ Icy surfaces could prove painful for small, wet hands or tongues. Remind your child never to touch.

❑ Keep small magnets off your fridge.

❑ Do not overload you electric sockets.

❑ Check all electric-appliance leads. Shorten leads or move any appliance that may cause an accident.

❑ Keep pet dishes away from small children and lift any unfinished food or water.

❑ Regularly check and maintain your child's high-chair, booster seat, or travel high-chair.

❑ Remove the table cloth from your table.

❑ Keep your bin in a locked cupboard.

❑ Never carry children and hot foods or drinks at the same time.

❑ If practical, install a safety-gate at the kitchen door to keep your child out.

❑ While loading and unloading your dishwasher, remove the cutlery tray first and replace it just before locking your machine.

CHAPTER THREE

BATHROOMS

A child's natural fondness for playing with water means the bathroom can be just as dangerous as the kitchen.

TOILET

To an adult the toilet is the last place you want as your child's playground. Unfortunately, children are fascinated by the swirling action the water makes when it is flushed and keeping your youngster away from it might prove difficult. Keep the toilet lid down at all times and place a toilet lock on it if possible. A toddler can easily fall in and drown. Never leave toilet cleaner to soak in the toilet.

Siobhan loved tea parties. And when she had them, which was frequently, everything had to be just perfect.

On her little table in her bedroom, the three-year-old would spread the tiny tablecloth her mum had made for her. She'd meticulously lay out the cups, saucers, teaspoons and side plates and in the middle she'd position a plate of pretend cakes. Siobhan preferred it when her mum let her have real biscuits and allowed her to fill the miniature teapot up with juice.

One afternoon Siobhan settled her dolls and little brother around her table. She begged her mum to join them and she eventually agreed to take part for just a moment as she was in the middle of doing the housework.

When her mum sat down, Siobhan had already poured out the tea for her brother who had already started drinking his. Mum immediately become suspicious about where the 'tea' had come from as she hadn't filled her daughter's teapot.

She asked Siobhan where it had come from, but all Siobhan would say was the kettle. Mum took a sniff of the 'tea' and, recognising the smell, immediately whisked the cups away from her children. Siobhan had filled her teapot from the toilet into which mum had earlier squirted some toilet cleaner and left it to soak.

Soibhan's little brother was kept under observation in hospital for a short while but fortunately he had not drunk enough of the 'tea' to do any real harm.

BATHTUB
Never under any circumstances leave a child under the age of five unsupervised in a bathtub. Drownings frequently happen quickly and silently, so do not think you will hear your child scream if he slips under the

water. Childhood drownings and near-drownings happen in a matter of seconds and typically happen when a child is left unattended or during a brief lapse of supervision.

Bathtime was a big treat for three-year-old Alan and his one-year-old sister Hannah. They loved their baths, especially when mum put in lots of bubbles so they could build big mountains and hide from each other behind them.

That particular evening, the children's father was away on business and their mum was left to bathe them by herself. Mum had been very busy at work and was behind in her household chores. She thought she'd give the upstairs a quick vacuum while the children played in the bath.

Within ten minutes Sandra was back in the bathroom to finish washing her children. As she walked into the bathroom, Alan excitedly showed her his bubble mountain he had built. But there was no sign of Hannah.

Frantically Sandra looked around the bathroom before she caught a glimpse of a strand of blond hair bobbing among the bubbles. Hannah was lying motionless at the bottom of the tub. Sandra yanked her daughter out of the tub and tried to resuscitate her before calling 999.

But it was too late; the paramedics were unable to revive her. Sandra thought that should Hannah slip under the bath, her three-year-old son would either help Hannah out of the water or shout for her.

Tragically, there is no safety in numbers. Young children are not always able to recognise when someone is in trouble.

Children may drown in as little as one inch of water and are therefore at risk of drowning in bathtubs, buckets, nappy pails, toilets and paddling pools. Never overfill a bathtub. If you use a nappy bucket make sure it has a locking lid. Immediately after using a bucket, empty it. Never leave anything to chance.

When bathing, keep at least one hand on your young child and always support an infant's head. Protect your child's eyes from shampoo and soap suds. Never be distracted by the telephone or doorbell, and remember kids are slippery when wet!

Here are some quick tips for tub safety:
- A baby's skin is more sensitive than yours. Always put cold water in first and top it up with hot.
- Mix the bath water so that it feels just warm and test the temperature of the water with your elbow or wrist never with your hand, as your hand quite often gives a false indication as to how hot the water is.
- Turn off water before putting your child in.
- Use a rubber bathmat in the tub to prevent slipping or falls.
- Use soft tap covers to prevent bumps and bruises.
- Never rely on older children to keep younger siblings safe from harm. Children do not always recognise when someone is in danger.
- If evening bathing is always a rushed, chaotic affair, consider switching it to a quieter period during the day when both you and your child will be much more relaxed.

TUB TEMPERATURES
Burns have long been recognised as among the most

painful and devastating injuries a human being can sustain and survive, so keep the water in your house set at about a hand-hot temperature to prevent scalds and burns.

Children under four years of age may scream and cry if the water in the bath is too hot but will not know to get out of it. Hot tap-water burns commonly occur when a child is left unattended in the bathtub, is placed in water that is too hot, is in the bathtub when another child turns on the hot water, or falls into the bathtub.

Young children have thinner skin than older children and adults and it will burn at lower temperatures and more deeply. A child exposed to very hot tap water could sustain a third-degree burn – an injury requiring hospitalisation and skin grafts. These can be prevented by lowering the setting on water heater thermostats.

The majority of bathtub scalding cases are due to the fact that a parent or childminder neglected to test the temperature of the bathwater before putting a child into it.

But in the case of eighteen-month-old Samuel, his mum Alison insists she tested the water before putting him in.

As usual, the 23-year-old mum ran a bath for her son then left him in the water while she went to make their evening meal. About half an hour later Alison went back upstairs to finish washing Samuel. She found him unconscious with severe burns all over his body.

Samuel was taken to hospital but was pronounced dead on arrival. The ensuing investigation queried how the bath water could have been so hot as to kill Samuel, but his mother insisted that he must have turned on the hot-water tap after she left the room.

GENERAL BATHROOM SAFETY TIPS

Check that sliding shower doors are made of safety glass and throw away soap when it reduces small enough to fit inside a child's mouth, roughly the size of a 50-pence piece. Children can, and have, choked to death on soap.

Little Jessica loved to play with her mum's make-up and every morning as her mum got ready for work Jessica would be nearby picking up the little pots and the brushes, eager to experiment. Depending on how rushed she was, Jessica's mum would sometimes let her daughter experiment.

This morning, Jessica's mum was in a hurry. The alarm clock did not go off and they had all overslept.

After quickly dressing Jessica and her two older sisters, Yvonne went into the bathroom to put on her make-up. As usual, 20-month-old Jessica was on her heels.

She was disappointed when her mum told her there was no time for her to play with the make-up. And after a short burst of temper, she started pottering about with the other bits and pieces that are typically found in a family bathroom.

Suddenly Jessica started choking. Her mum grabbed her daughter and put her over her knees, slapping her on the back. But to no avail. Yvonne kept it up until Jessica stopped choking and went blue. Prying open her daughter's mouth to see if she could fish out whatever it was that her daughter had put in her mouth, Yvonne spotted a small piece of soap jammed in her throat. She lay Jessica on the floor and tried to scoop it out with her fingers, but its so slippery that it slid even further down her daughters throat.

Yvonne shouted for one of her older daughters to dial 999 and get an ambulance quickly.

Jessica was lucky to survive. Doctors retrieved the small piece of soap about the size of a 50-pence piece from her throat.

Choking is one of the easiest ways for a child to die. Hardly a day goes by without a hospital emergency room treating a child which is either choking or has stuffed something up its nose.

The main culprits tend to be coins. However emergency room nurses will say it's amazing the number of things a child will put in their mouths or noses. They also report that what's particularly life-threatening is when children actually inhale small lightweight items that they have put in their mouths, such as drawing pins and paper clips, into their lungs which results in emergency surgery.

Remember to keep all electrical appliances away from water. A person can receive a nasty shock if an appliance, such as a radio, falls into the bath or shower even when not switched on.

Keep bathroom appliances unplugged and stored well out of reach of little hands. It is also a good idea to keep your child out of the bathroom when you are getting ready.

Even a simple item like a toothbrush can cause a child severe harm if he trips and falls while one is in his mouth.

Keep sharp objects such as razors, razor blades and nail clippers and scissors stored safely away.

If you must have a lock on the door, a stiff bolt placed high up on the door is less likely to result in your child locking himself in.

MEDICINES

All medications should be kept in a locked and secure place. Just putting medications on a high shelf is not enough. Children can be very ingenious when they want something. It's also a good idea to keep medicine boxes out of sight as well as out of reach.

Make sure all medicines are stored in child-resistant and shatter-proof containers, and do not save old prescription medicines – flush them down the toilet when you are finished using them. The less medication you have in the house the safer your family will be.

Never tell your child that medicine tastes 'like sweeties' or is good. It's better to have to struggle to get them to take it.

Store children's vitamins in a safe place too, as a child can overdose on them.

If your child does swallow any medicine, get whatever you can out of his mouth and call 999 immediately. Have the bottle in your hand so you can tell the emergency operator what was ingested and approximately how much.

WASTE-BASKET

Never throw used razor blades, toothbrushes and other potentially dangerous materials such as creams, lotions or ointments into the bathroom's waste-basket. Children love to rummage and your bathroom's bin will be just like a treasure chest to him if you allow it.

Remember not to throw ear buds in the waste-basket either. Children love to mimic and may stick it too far down the ear canal and puncture an eardrum.

CHECKLIST

❑ Never leave a young child alone in the bath. A child can drown in an inch of water.

❑ Empty all buckets immediately after use and keep the nappy-pail lid firmly locked.

❑ Always keep one hand on a very young child while bathing them – children are slippery when wet.

❑ Always fill the bath with cold water first then top it up with hot water until it is warm. Test the water temperature with your wrist or elbow only.

❑ Never let your child into a bath without a rubber bathmat.

❑ Hot tap water can seriously burn. Keep your household water at a hand-hot temperature.

❑ Check shower doors are made of safety glass.

❑ Throw away soap when it is roughly the size of a 50p piece. It is a choking hazard.

❑ Keep all electrical appliances out of the bathroom.

❑ Keep all medicines in a locked cabinet or box, out of sight and out of reach of children.

❑ Never let your child play with a toothbrush.

❑ Never throw used razor blades, medications or ear buds in the bathroom's waste-basket.

❑ Don't leave bleach or other chemicals soaking in your toilet.

CHAPTER FOUR

THE LIVING-ROOM

As the name suggests families, along with their friends and relatives, spend a great deal of time in this room which is why it's very important to thoroughly baby-proof it. Keep a constant look out for new, dropped or forgotten items that could easily become a hazard.

Mums – make sure you keep your handbags and purses out of reach as keys, coins, cosmetics and medication or anything else you keep inside are not playthings for your child. Pay attention to visitors too. Remind them there is a baby or young child in the house and put their coats and handbags out of reach. Watch for loose change that may fall out of men's pockets.

Smoking in a home where a child is present is very dangerous. Secondary smoke can affect a child's lung capacity. If you choose to continue smoking after a baby comes home from the hospital never hold a lit cigarette while handling a child. Put away your ash-trays and be very conscious of where you leave matches and lighters.

Two-year-old Josh was fascinated by his parents smoking and like most kids he liked to imitate his parents' actions.

One afternoon Josh spied his mum's packet of cigarettes lying on top of the sideboard in the dining-room. He grabbed the packet, opened it and pulled a few out.

Instead of pretending to smoke the cigarette, Josh put them in his mouth and started to eat them. That was when his mum walked into the room and caught him with a mouthful of tobacco. She wiped what she could from his mouth before scolding him.

A few minutes later a friend of Josh's mum called round. Elizabeth told her friend what she had just caught Josh eating. Her friend told her that eating cigarettes could kill a child.

Elizabeth had no idea how many or how much Josh had actually swallowed and took him to hospital where he was treated for nicotine poisoning. Josh was all right but Elizabeth was shocked to hear from nurses that just one cigarette for every year of the child's age could prove fatal.

Do not leave family heirlooms and other valuable or sentimental ornaments and objects on display. Do not clear shelves and tables of everything though. By leaving a few sturdy, inexpensive objects out you can teach your child they are not his playthings by telling him not to touch every time he gets near it. It will not be long before your child learns not to touch 'mummy's things' and you will be able to surround yourself with your favourite things once more.

Check all of your home's fitted carpets for loose staples or nails and repair where necessary.

Do not allow your children to leave toys lying all over the floor. It's an accident waiting to happen and never let your child run around with objects in his mouth.

It was a wet Saturday afternoon. Josh's mum was out doing the weekly shop and his dad was watching football on the telly.

Seven-year-old Josh was restless. He wanted to play outside but his dad had said no. Eventually Josh's dad, desperate for some peace to watch the game, set Josh up at the kitchen table with some coloured pencils and paper to draw a picture for mummy.

This proved only a mild distraction for Josh who quickly grew bored and decided on another game. He stuck two of the coloured pencils in his mouth and pretended to be dracula.

As Josh ran around the living-room, he suddenly tripped on a toy that had been left lying on the floor and fell flat on his face. One of the pencils, fell out of his mouth before he hit the floor; the other one which he had put in his mouth sharp side up imbedded itself in the roof of his mouth.

FURNITURE

Take a close look at all of the furniture in your living-room. It should be anchored down as your child will view every piece as a Munro to bag. Each year, children are severely injured or killed by unsecured furniture which has toppled on to them when they tried to climb or pull themselves up on it. These include bookshelves, chests of drawers, television trolleys, stands or tables. Secure them to the wall and clear away breakables.

> Two-year-old Adrian was crushed to death when a chest of drawers he had been climbing on toppled over. The youngster's head was caught in the bottom drawer with the rest of his body trapped underneath the piece of furniture.
>
> Adrian was found by his ten-year-old brother, Euan, after being left alone in a bedroom for a few minutes at his grandparents' home.

Another two-year-old boy was killed when a chest of drawers he and his twin brother had been playing on toppled over.

> Brett and Brian had been put down for a nap by their mother while she did some housework. When she went to check on the twins a short time later she found one unconscious under the chest. Apparently the twins had been playing and managed to open the drawers despite the fact that safety-catches had been installed to prevent them from doing exactly that. The dresser toppled over and caught the child beneath it.

* * *

Four-year-old Jimmy was riding his tricycle through the house when he went into his parents' study. The front wheel of the trike struck the leg of a computer table which collapsed sending the computer, monitor and printer crashing to the ground. Jimmy was very lucky. He escaped with a broken leg and some minor cuts and bruises.

* * *

A brother and sister aged three and four were seriously injured when they climbed onto a six-foot-high bookcase. The bookcase toppled over onto both children who were hospitalised with multiple broken bones.

* * *

While giving her dining-room a good vacuuming, a mother piled the dining-room chairs on to the table. Her young daughter climbed on to them, causing the unstable load to crash all around her. The young girl escaped with a broken shoulder and arm.

Television tip-overs are particularly serious. Always place your television on low furniture and as far back as possible.

Four-year-old Jason was playing in the living-room while his baby-sitter, Sarah, fixed them both a snack in the kitchen.

Jason's mum and dad had gone to the cinema for a late-afternoon matinee. As they didn't go out very often, it was a treat for Jason too, to spend some time with his favourite baby-sitter.

Sarah had helped Jason build a zoo with his Lego kit on the floor in a corner of the living-room. As they did this, the satellite played endless cartoons on the television.

From where Jason was sitting, he was finding it difficult to see the television set easily. He walked across the room and tried to adjust the set to a better viewing position.

The 27-inch television sat on a wheeled trolley-type stand in the corner of the room. As Jason pulled at the cart, it gave a sudden lunge and sent the giant television toppling off the stand.

He gave a loud shriek as he hit the floor with the television pinning him down. Sarah ran out of the kitchen and found Jason unconscious on the floor.

Jason survived just a few days in hospital but later died of severe head injuries.

Make sure any television set – no matter what size – is located on a firm and stable piece of furniture, preferably a low piece to prevent children climbing on to it and toppling it over, and push the television well back.

Pad any sharp edges with cushioned corner guards. Check under tables and chairs and anything else your baby could crawl under. Get down on hands and knees yourself and crawl about the room looking for exposed nails, staples and screws. If any tables have tablecloths get rid of them as babies love to pull on them.

Old lead-based paint is a highly toxic poison. You need to check for it on furniture and walls and have it removed

Check your cabinet and unit drawers. If they contain items unsuitable for your child to play with install a safety-catch which not only prevents curious fingers from playing with these items but it also stops drawers from being pulled out on top of your little explorer. Tighten any loose drawer or cabinet knobs, too.

FIREPLACES, RADIATORS, GAS AND ELECTRIC HEATERS

Thousands of children aged four years and under are burned every year by domestic fires and heaters in the home. Fireplaces, gas and electric heaters should all have protective fire-guards placed round them. Never leave a child unattended in a room with a burning open fire, even if it has a fire-guard. There is no safety substitution for a parent's wary eye.

Do not ignore radiators and hot air registers either. Keep temperatures down to avoid burns and watch a child if he is playing near one. It is another area where you want to teach your little one the meaning of the words 'No' and 'Hot'.

Little Gemma was fascinated by fire engines, police cars and ambulances. She loved the noise their sirens made as they raced along the road.

One evening after her bath, Gemma was downstairs having a drink of milk before going to bed when a fire engine, its sirens blaring, raced past the house. Gemma ran from the kitchen in to the living-room where she climbed onto a low table beneath the front window to try and see it going past.

As the 18-month-old tot leaned forward to get a better view, her tummy pressed against the radiator. Although she was in pain and started screaming, little children do not always instinctively know to pull away from something that is hurting them.

The toddler's thin pyjamas offered no protection from the radiator which was so hot it left an exact imprint of itself on her abdomen.

Gemma's parents' quick thinking, doctors later said, prevented the wound from continuing to burn her flesh by applying bags of frozen vegetables wrapped in a damp tea-towel to her abdomen.

BABY-WALKERS

A baby-walker should only ever be used on a smooth surface. Carpet edges, rugs, or raised areas and steps could cause a walker to tip over.

Remove rugs when your baby is in his walker and block off stairs. Children have fallen down stairs in walkers and have either been seriously injured or died.

PLAYPENS

A playpen is a great safety aid when used occasionally, but do not put your child in one all day. It will slow down your child's natural exploration and environmental stimulation.

Never tie a toy across the top of a playpen when a

child is old enough to push himself onto his hands and knees or when he reaches five months old, whichever comes first. A child could fall onto it or his neck could get tangled or twisted in the string and strangle himself.

Mesh playpens and travel cots should never be used with a side left down as it could pose a serious hazard to newborns and young babies as the mesh forms a loose pocket into which an infant could roll and suffocate.

The sides should be high enough to contain an 18-month-old child, and should have no more than two inches (five centimetres) between the bars.

Be sure your child cannot lower the side of the playpen by himself.

ELECTRIC SHOCKS

Its a sad fact of life that children are commonly electrocuted through household electric sockets. Modern square-pin sockets are a lot safer since a child can't poke an object into the bottom holes unless something goes into the top hole too – something a determined child will figure out eventually. So it's worthwhile to invest in socket covers which are inexpensive and one of the easiest safety products to install in your home.

A child's natural curiosity to stick things into dark holes means sockets are an easy lure. And the results could be catastrophic.

Fiona loved it when her parents had parties, despite the fact she was always put to bed early.

Once the guests had arrived and were settled, Fiona would quietly get out of her bed and creep to the top landing where she would listen for hours to her parents and guests chattering.

Sometimes, if she was feeling particularly brave, she would creep downstairs, and grab a handful or crisps or *hors d'oeuvres* from the kitchen when nobody was around. Even if she wasn't hungry or she didn't particularly like what she had grabbed she did it because it was part of the thrill.

One night, Fiona was feeling adventurous and did creep downstairs into the kitchen. But before she got the chance to snatch any goodies, her mum came out of the living-room and Fiona bolted back upstairs. But not before she grabbed a souvenir of her trip downstairs – a shiny silver fork.

Fiona resumed her perch at the top of the stairs. The party wasn't very exciting and she began to get bored, then she spotted the electric socket.

She crawled over to it and poked the prongs into the socket. Suddenly there was a loud bang and a flash and Fiona was sent flying backwards.

Her parents and their guests came running into the hall to see what happened. There was Fiona, thankfully only shaken and stunned, lying on the floor quite a few feet from the socket. Since the fork was still in the socket, her parents immediately knew what had happened. They called out the emergency doctor who pronounced that Fiona was fine.

He also told her shocked parents that Fiona probably got away lightly because she was wearing rubber-soled slippers.

Other electrical dangers in the living-room include power cables. Children love to chew on them and they are especially fun to tug on. But the game will have tragic consequences if there is a heavy lamp on the other end of the cable.

Make sure all power cables are held in place behind heavy furniture or are firmly stapled or taped to the floor or walls. Also keep cables clear of high traffic areas to prevent trips and falls.

Replace any frayed or worn cables – especially if any bare wire is showing through – and use cord shorteners to tidy up loose wires. A mere 12 inches of cable is all it takes to choke a child.

Do not put cables or flexes under carpet and rugs as a worn one might start a fire.

Unplug and put away items such as fans, irons and electric or gas heaters when not in use. And make sure there is a light bulb in every lamp socket in the house. Curious fingers poked in here could result in a nasty shock.

> Marie was vacuuming her bedroom with her new multi-coloured vacuum cleaner when the motor suddenly spluttered and stopped. She tried the power switch several times to try and get it started again before going into the hallway to check the plug.
>
> Marie saw her 22-month-old son with the sweeper's bright yellow plug pulled halfway out from the socket with his fingers about to wrap round the plug's metal prongs in order to pull it out further.
>
> Marie screamed at him 'No' just in time to prevent her son electrocuting himself.

Multi-coloured plugs might brighten up an otherwise dull electric lead but parents should remember that they can also prove too attractive to youngsters.

BALCONIES

If you live in a flat and have a balcony you must take extra care that your child cannot climb over the edge. Ensure railings have a gap no bigger than four inches between them. If there is any pattern to the railings that might be used as a climbing frame, board it up or cover the area with fine chicken wire to prevent your child from getting a foothold.

Ban any furniture or potted plants that your child might use to help him climb up.

DRINKS CABINETS

All alcohol must be locked well away from curious little children. If you are enjoying an evening drink do not put it down where your child could reach it. Alcohol is a deadly poison to children.

After a party, do not go to bed until every bottle and glass is cleared away. It would be tragic if your youngster got to them before you did in the morning.

> It was Christmas Eve and the Evans' household was full of Yuletide cheer. Throughout the day, family and friends had stopped by to leave presents for the three young children.
>
> Eighteen-month-old Josh was the middle one of the three boys. They were all very excited over the

expectation of Santa coming that night, and the sight of all those extra presents being put under their Christmas tree was almost unbearable.

In all the excitement, nobody saw Josh toddle over to a side table where an unfinished glass of whisky stood. And nobody saw as Josh downed the glass's entire contents as if it was orange juice.

It didn't take long for the whisky to have an effect on the youngster and very soon he was staggering about and vomiting. Josh's mum quickly figured out what her son had done and took him to hospital where doctors monitored him closely, particularly in case he choked on his own vomit. Eventually they allowed Josh's mum to take him home, safe in the knowledge that the only side-effect that her youngster would suffer would be a bad hangover the next day.

In another part of the country that same Christmas Eve a young, single mum was throwing a party for her friends and neighbours. Her six-year-old daughter was helping her mum play hostess – passing round bowls of crisps and other food.

Sharon thought her daughter Kylie was so grown up, especially the way she chatted freely and easily with her friends. Sharon didn't think a glass of wine would hurt when Kylie asked if she could have one.

But it did. That single glass of wine killed her daughter who choked to death on her own vomit.

PARTIES

Children's birthday parties can be great fun for everybody if a little thought and preparation goes into the event.

If it's to be an indoor party, limit it to one room only and childproof that room as carefully as you possibly can. Leave nothing to chance. What your child might not have thought of doing, you can count on another one thinking of and doing it.

Remove any portable electrical appliances and everything breakable from the room to be used.

Block off any exits with gates, if possible. Keep a path clear to the toilet and a nappy-changing area, but be sure other rooms are not easily accessible to your child's playmates.

Keep the front door locked, opening it only for guests. Insist that the children leave this for an adult to do.

As soon as the candles on the birthday cake are lit, put the matches away.

For your guests' safety as well as your pets', banish your dog or cat to a safe room.

Do not serve small sweets, peanuts, popcorn, grapes or raisins. In all the excitement of the party, a child could easily choke on one of these.

If small children will be at the party, forget using a tablecloth. The risk of having hot food, sharp knives, glasses and heavy bowls pulled on to little heads is too great.

If the party is for very young children then make sure you invite their parents as well.

Depending on the age group and number of children at the party, at least two adults should be supervising. Accidents happen when everyone thinks someone else is watching the kids. And do not let children run around while eating.

If the party is outdoors on a summer's day keep foods that may spoil in a cool spot. Salads and meats left out at parties can cause food poisoning.

Keep your eyes on glasses and bottles of alcohol left around. Children may imitate the adults by drinking the alcohol left in the bottom of a glass or bottle. Dump any drinks left around and lock up any bottles that are not in use.

If a barbecue is to be used at the party, it must be attended by an adult at all times.

At least one parent at the party must remain sober to supervise the children. A little-known law is that it is illegal to be in charge of children while under the influence of alcohol.

If your guests are tired or drunk, do not let them drive home, especially if they have children.

CHECKLIST

❑ Always look for dropped or forgotten items that could harm your child.

❑ Keep purses and handbags out of your child's reach.

❑ Watch out for loose change that may fall out of pockets.

❑ Never smoke in the same room as a child.

❑ Keep all rooms clear of cigarettes, lighters, and ashtrays.

❑ Do not leave expensive or sentimental items on display.

❑ Check carpets for loose nails or staples.

❑ Anchor all furniture that could topple on to your child.

❑ Place televisions on low furniture that cannot easily fall over.

❑ Keep on the lookout for sharp edges, exposed nails, tapes and screws on furniture.

❑ Make sure your fire has a guard.

❑ Never let your baby play alone in a babywalker.

❑ Never tie toys across the tops of playpens.

❑ Never leave a playpen's side down.

❑ Fit socket covers to all power points.

❑ Secure all power cables out of your child's reach.

❑ Keep bulbs in light fixtures.

❑ Keep all alcohol out of your child's reach.

❑ Before a party remove electrical appliances and breakables from the room.

❑ Keep pets away from guests.

❑ Do not use tablecloths.

❑ Do not give young children foods that can be easily choked on.

❑ Enforce party rules – like no running while eating.

❑ Never leave a barbecue unattended.

❑ Do not let parents get drunk and drive a child home.

❑ Keep radiator temperatures down low.

❑ Child-proof your balcony.

CHAPTER FIVE

DOORS, WINDOWS AND STAIRS

It's a child's job to be a lot of things but being inquisitive gets top billing. Numerous bumps and bruises are the usual pay-off during their quest to sate their natural curiosity. But occasionally the pay-off is a lot worse if adequate safeguards are not employed by a parent.

Statistics show that children up to the age of ten are at the greatest risk of injuries from falls as they develop co-ordination and other motor skills. Generally these falls are from furniture, stairs, windows and playground equipment. A large proportion of non-fatal home accidents are due to falls. In 1995, 371,998 accidents were due to falls. Of these, almost 60,000 children under the age of five were injured falling down the stairs.

Furniture, stairs and baby-walkers are the danger zone areas for babies, while windows pose the biggest threat to toddlers. Older children tend to suffer more from falls from playground equipment.

It is not surprising to hear that more than 80 per cent of fall-related injuries among children aged four and under happen at home because that is the place children of this age group spend the majority of their time.

Nobody would argue that a parent could prevent every one of their child's falls. But what is sad is when you pick up a newspaper and read about a toddler that has fallen out of a window or off a balcony, because, while nobody expects a parent to keep a constant vigil on their youngster's every move, there are some simple and inexpensive safeguards a parent can take to prevent such catastrophic accidents.

DOORS AND LOCKS

To your child every door is this wonderful, magical gateway into a new and exciting place just waiting for him to explore. Walk around your house and try to look at it through your child's eyes.

As the grown-up you will know exactly what lies on the other side of every door in your home. That door to the balcony might offer wonderful panoramic views of the city, but it also offers certain death if your toddler were to tumble over the edge.

The door to your bedroom might seem just like any door to you but to your child it's a fabulous opportunity to hunt for treasure in mummy's jewellery box, dress up, jump on the bed, or a million other things including sampling some of those 'sweets' mummy takes every day and never offers anybody.

The bathroom door opens up the opportunity for water play, either in the sink, bathtub or even the toilet – not to mention the fun you could have playing imaginary sword-fights with the toilet brush or sampling all the contents of the multitude of jars and bottles most bathrooms have.

The doors leading outside are even better. In this light

many parents can see the valuable reasoning for installing locks around the house. Every door that opens to the outside world should always stay closed and locked when not in use. Toddlers can operate an ordinary door handle, so watch out if your door is easy to open. Install a tricky or stiff catch or rig up a loud bell that rings every time the door opens.

Inside the house any door leading to a stairway or room that is off-limits to a young child should have a lock fitted. The most practical latches are the kind that can be opened by adults from either side of the door, though a simple hook and eye works too. Latches should be positioned at least five feet high, while slide locks can be used on cabinet doors.

Bathroom and bedroom doors present a special problem. In many homes they can be locked only from inside the room. This creates the risk of not being able to reach a child in trouble. These locks should be removed or a key hung outside the door so a parent can quickly access a room that a child has locked himself in to.

Some parents turn their child's bedroom door around so that the lock is on the outside. Others take this one step further and cut the door in half so that it resembles a stable door. The bottom half can be locked, perhaps to keep in a child who will not stay in his bedroom at bedtime, and the top half can be opened so that the child does not feel isolated and locked in. This is a particularly good idea if there are areas of your home where your child might harm himself if he were to get up during the night and wander round unsupervised.

Glass doors need to be made of safety glass, or the glass should be covered with a special safety adhesive. This type of plastic film, which becomes invisible once its fitted, will help prevent glass from shattering all over your child in the event of an accident. Put brightly coloured stickers at child-height on glass doors to reduce the risk of your child running into them.

Do not forget that locks and latches only work when you use them. Install them as soon as the baby comes home from hospital. That gives your family time to get into the habit of closing and locking doors.

Give serious consideration to padded door-jambs that can be bought from any store that sells child-safety equipment.

Three-year-old Declan liked the power and influence he had over his year-old brother. Andrew would naively do almost anything his older brother told him to.

One of his favourite games was making Andrew put his fingers in the gap between the door and the frame and then slowly closing it until Andrew screamed in pain. On one occasion he did it so hard as to severely bruise one of Andrew's fingers; the nail later turned black and fell off.

Andrew was lucky. A sad fact of life is the number of severed finger tips that are brought into hospital accident departments as a result of a door being closed on them.

* * *

Three-year-old Claire was messing about in the back of the car as her dad Neil put Claire's younger sister in her car seat in the front. When he finished strapping the infant in, he slammed the car door shut firmly.

Claire immediately started screaming. Her dad could not understand why. She was standing in the back seat footwell and he could see nothing wrong with her. He kept asking what was wrong until Claire managed to get the words out that her fingers were 'stuck'.

It took a few moments before Neil realised that he had unwittingly slammed Claire's fingers in the door. His daughter had been clutching the door frame at the time.

Neil quickly opened the door and found that the tip of Claire's finger was barely attached. Wrapping her finger tightly in a handkerchief he drove straight to hospital where, fortunately, doctors were able to reattach it.

WINDOWS

Windows are the eye to the world for young children but pose a monumental safety threat. A baby can squirm through a tiny gap of less than five inches – to the untrained eye that does not appear a big enough space for your precious bundle to squeeze through, but it is. Every window that is not on ground level should have window catches or locks fitted. Many parents also put them on ground-floor windows too.

Remember that the majority of window falls happen during spring and summer months when the good weather proves too much of a temptation to air the house. Children living in flats are particularly at risk.

Remember to cut or tie-up all curtain and blind cords to prevent your child strangling himself. If you have sharp-edged venetian blinds it might be a good idea to remove them.

If possible avoid putting furniture under windows. The harder it is for your child to access a window the less likely it is that he will fall out of it.

It is also very important to make sure you can quickly and easily unlock windows in case of a fire. Keep keys next to the window, but out of children's reach. Some people even tape keys high up on the frame.

Stairs

Through a baby's eyes every set of stairs is a chance to scale Everest. And as every child is a born explorer he will go at it with dogged determination.

Stair gates are a must in the early days, preferably one at both the top and the bottom of a stairway. Never use pressure gates at the top of stairs as a child could push through it and fall down the stairs. Neither should you use any accordion-style gate which could pinch fingers or even trap your child's head. There are many types on the market but if you are choosing one for the top of a stairway make sure it screws into the wall for extra strength and ensure the gap between the gate and the floor is less than two inches.

If you put a gate at the bottom of your stairs, leave two or three steps free so your baby can practise climbing on them. When your child is old enough, spend time teaching him how to climb up and down.

Banisters should be sturdy with less than four inches between the posts. If the gaps are any larger than that your baby could get his head or neck caught and suffocate or could even fall right through. If you have found that your banisters have large gaps you will need to board them up. Also, if your banister has any horizontal slats in it, you will have to board it up too to stop children from using it as a ladder.

Stairs are not meant to be an extra storage area. Anything placed on the stairs can become an obstacle to fall over. If you are one of those people who pile things up on the stairs waiting to be carried on the next trip up, now is a good time to break that bad habit. If constant going up and down the stairs seems too much like hard work, then leave a sturdy box in the hallway ready to collect these items.

Make sure repairs are carried out immediately on any loose stairs, carpets or railings.

Rugs that do not have non-slip backings should be avoided anywhere in the house but particularly at the top or bottom of stairs as the risk of slipping is too great.

Use a nightlight in the hallway for children who get up in the night.

COMMUNAL LANDINGS

If you live in a block of flats with a communal landing you will probably discover that the gaps between railings in the stairwell and on the landing do not afford much protection to a youngster. If this is the case, do not let your child use the stairs by himself. It would be far too easy for him to slip through the gaps if you are not there.

CHECKLIST

❑ Put brightly coloured stickers on glass doors so your child will not run into them.

❑ Patio doors need special locks at the top to stop your child sneaking out.

❑ Watch out for little fingers when closing doors.

❑ Attach a bell to a door so you can hear it opening.

❑ Remember that all doors – front, back, bathroom or kitchen – can pose a hazard. Keep them closed and locked where possible.

❑ Install window locks or adjust them so they cannot open more than five inches (12 centimetres).

❑ Tie up or cut curtain and blind pull-cords so your child will not get tangled up in them.

❑ Install safety glass or adhesive in large windows and glass doors so they will not shatter if a child falls into them.

❑ Do not leave furniture or anything that can be climbed upon near a window. Consider installing window locks on all windows, ground floor as well as upstairs. Make sure keys for all locks are kept near windows and within adult reach in case of a fire.

❑ Install a safety gate at the top and bottom of stairways.

❑ Never leave anything on the stairs that you could trip on while carrying your baby, and do not carry too much.

❑ Take keys out of doors that lock on the inside and store nearby out of children's reach.

❑ Make sure all rugs have non-slip backings and keep them away from stairs or the front of glass doors or large glass windows.

❑ Carry out repairs immediately on loose railings, stairs, broken windows or banisters.

❑ Ensure main doors leading out of your home have tricky locks or stiff catches.

❑ Your child can lock himself in the bathroom – consider removing the lock and placing a bolt high on the door.

❑ If young children get up in the night, install a nightlight in the hall.

❑ If you live in a flat with a communal landing, check the gaps between railings as well as any window fixtures or locks.

CHAPTER SIX

THE NURSERY

The nursery is often the first room excited parents-to-be will start putting together. Usually, a lot of time is spent picking co-ordinating wallpapers, curtains and bedding. But this time would be better spent searching for and choosing the safest furniture and toys as the nursery is where your baby will sleep and play, and it is a place where he should be totally safe. A safe nursery also gives you peace of mind.

Start from scratch and empty everything that can be removed out of the room. Check the door for peeling paint or rough patches. Does it lock on the inside? If so put the key in a safe place, outside the room but near the door. Do windows have locks or guards on them to prevent a baby tumbling out of the window? Are wardrobes sturdy and in good condition? Chests of drawers should also be sturdy and without sharp edges.

As you decorate and fill the room with furniture and objects, double-check that each item is safe for your baby. It's a good practice to start as you mean to go on.

A word about purchasing baby furniture and

equipment. If you plan to buy it second-hand, make sure the equipment is in good condition and meets up-to-date safety standards. Check with your local trading standards office or contact the British Standards Agency or RoSPA for details. Check to see that a product is right for your child's age and size and follow instructions and safety tips. Thoroughly check furniture construction – it should be stable, not able to be easily tipped and have no sharp edges or corners. Test safety straps – are they strong and easy to use? Is the product made from quality materials, without sharp edges or parts? Will it stand up to rough treatment? Are there small parts than can be easily detached and swallowed? Check for loose staples, screws, nuts and bolts, and regularly inspect equipment for wear and tear.

Cots

Be aware of the risks of cot death and check on your child regularly. Always put your child down to sleep on his back. Never lie him in his cot on his stomach unless under medical advice.

One of the most important pieces of nursery furniture is the cot. Place it away from draughts and radiators or hot-air registers. Do not put it near a window where full sunlight filtering through an open window can burn sensitive skins.

Today's cots and mattresses must meet stringent safety standards but, again, check that second-hand equipment complies with these standards.

There should be a gap of no more than two inches (five centimetres) between cot bars so a baby's body cannot fit through the bars or trap his head, with the distance from the top rail to the mattress being a minimum of 20 inches

(50 centimetres). Mattresses should fit snugly, so a baby cannot get trapped between the mattress and the side of the cot; as well as having a mattress support that does not easily pull apart from the corner posts so a baby cannot get trapped between mattress and cot.

No corner posts over a sixteenth of an inch (one millimetre) above the end panels should be allowed (unless they are over 16 inches (41 centimetres) high for a canopy), so a baby cannot catch its clothing and strangle.

Ensure your baby cannot operate the locks on the cot's dropside and keep any stickers or transfers on the outside of the cot in case your baby peels them off and eats them.

When using second-hand cots check for chipped or peeling paint to prevent lead poisoning and splinters or sharp edges.

Keep cot sides in the raised position when the cot is in use and make sure your baby cannot reach the release latch.

Do not use pillows and duvets for babies under a year old. Pillows can suffocate a child of this age, as can duvets. Duvets can also cause a baby to overheat dangerously. Large soft toys, or numerous smaller ones, should also be kept out of the cot as they can also cause suffocation.

As your child grows, avoid bulky toys that could be used to climb up on and out to freedom. Bumpers can also provide an easy foothold for children trying to climb out. Nothing, including hanging mobiles, should be reachable from inside the cot.

Twenty-two-month-old Callum had turned into a real handful. It wasn't that he was naughty, just into everything. It seemed to his parents that it was only yesterday their quiet non-adventurous child had become a mini-Houdini.

That night they put their exhausted child to bed and they did not expect to hear a peep from him. Then they went downstairs to watch some television.

It wasn't long before their viewing was interrupted by a loud bang which seemed to come from the nursery.

Callum's parents found their son lying the floor beside his cot. It appeared he had piled soft toys against the side of the cot's bars and climbed out. The tot had broken one of his legs as a result of the fall. Doctors told Callum's mum and dad he was lucky as it could easily have been his neck that was broken instead of his leg.

Never use thin plastic material, such as cling-film or carrier bags, to cover mattresses or pillows as the plastic film can cling to a child's face causing suffocation.

IN THE ROOM

Baby-listeners are a wonderful invention for parents who can relax in another room or in the garden and still be able to listen out for their baby. However, they are not a substitute for watching your baby and you should still check in on a child. Check the batteries regularly.

Check all nursery equipment for exposed screws, bolts or fasteners with sharp edges or points and avoid scissor-like mechanisms which could crush fingers and avoid cut-out designs that could trap a child's head.

Use baby-walkers only on smooth surfaces – the edge

of carpets, rugs, or raised thresholds can cause a walker to tip over. Remove rugs when a walker is in use and block the top of stairs. Children have fallen down stairs in walkers.

Do not hang objects with strings or elastics (toys or laundry bags, for example) around cots or playpens when your child might become entangled and choke to death.

When children begin to climb and explore, they can become caught in small or narrow openings. Some have been strangled when they have caught their heads or necks in the open 'V' shapes in expandable wooden gets or enclosures, or in decorative cut-outs in older cots.

DUMMIES

Never tie dummies or other items around your baby's neck.

Cords and ribbons can become tightly twisted or can catch on cot cornerposts or other protrusions, and strangle your baby.

Two-year-old Oliver was a page boy at his Uncle Scott's wedding. As the ceremony was being held in London, Uncle Scott, who is a Scot, was determined that wherever possible, Highland dress was to be worn.

Oliver's mum rose to the occasion and completely kitted out her son in full Highland dress in his own family tartan. He almost stole the show as he walked down the aisle clutching the hand of three-year-old bridesmaid Grace.

As the wedding guests gathered after the ceremony in the nearby gardens for photographs, the children raced about letting out pent-up excitement that they had miraculously subdued during the ceremony.

Oliver found the dummy his mother had put inside his sporran and promptly popped it into his mouth. He then joined the other children in their game of tag. As they all raced about screaming and laughing, Oliver tripped over something lying on the ground and hurtled face first into the grass. Oliver's daddy quickly picked the youngster up, but Oliver's screams were more than the normal cries he gave out when he bumped himself and Oliver's daddy knew he must have hurt himself quite badly. He witnessed the fall and knew he'd probably hurt his mouth. The dummy had already fallen out of the youngster's mouth and the blood was beginning to pour from the gums above his front teeth.

Had the dummy not been in his mouth, Oliver would probably have suffered nothing more than a bumped head. Unfortunately the ground where Oliver fell was quite firm and the dummy smashed against Oliver's front teeth, fracturing them at the roots.

CURTAINS AND BLINDS

Pull-cords for curtains and blinds are very dangerous and frequent killers of children under the age of five.

The younger victims, usually between 10 and 15 months of age typically have been placed in a cot or playpen which has been placed near curtains or blinds.

Older children, usually from two to four years old, find cords hanging near the floor or have become twisted in cords while climbing on furniture to look out of the window. Entanglement and strangulation can occur when a child is alone in a room for only a short time.

For all blinds and curtains cut the cords to their shortest length possible. If this is not possible, tie the cords up near the top of the curtain rail, well out of your child's reach. And keep checking that it does not come undone.

CHANGING TABLES AND NAPPIES

Look for a table that is sturdily built. As soon as babies start to wriggle they can roll off on to the floor below. The safest place to change a baby is on the floor.

Keep all your nappy-changing supplies at hand as well as out of baby's reach. Never leave a child unattended for a second.

If you keep a nappy pail in the nursery be sure it has a locking lid. If it does not, keep it where your child cannot get to it. Young children can topple into the pail and drown.

Babies can pull the wadding and plastic tags off disposable nappies which can present a choking hazard if your child decides to eat them. A pair of plastic pants over the top should help deter your baby from doing this.

Store all chemicals, such as those used for cleaning terry nappies, disinfectants for changing mats or potties well out of your child's reach.

Talcum powder can cause babies to choke. It's really worth avoiding it.

BABY-BOUNCER SEATS

Your baby-bouncer seat should have a wide base, non-skid

bottom and a crotch and waist safety strap. Use a head support like those used in car seats to support an infant's head. A rolled towel placed carefully around the head will also protect his head from lolling. Do not put a bouncy seat on top of a table or worktop as it can, and frequently does, fall off. Never use one of these seats as a car seat.

INFANT SWINGS

Never leave your baby unattended in one of these swings. Use a head support for infants. Be careful your baby's head does not get caught between the edge of the back-rest and the bars from which the seat hangs. Protect your baby from falls.

TOY CHESTS

If a toy chest, trunk or other container for storing toys has a free-falling lid, remove the lid. A lid can drop on a child's head or neck which can seriously injure or kill your child. Choose a toy box which has sturdy supports to hold the lid open in any position or, better still, a lightweight removable lid. Look out for hinges that could pinch little fingers. If your child's toy box is large enough for your child to climb into and it has a tight-fitting lid, it might be a good idea to drill holes in the sides for ventilation in case your child gets trapped.

> Eleven-month-old Euan was playing alone in the nursery. He loved it in there and would often quite happily spend up to an hour alone in his room with all his toys.
> It was a welcome break for his mum Eileen who

was pregnant with twins. On this day she was having a rest on the sofa and watching some daytime television. She nodded off briefly and woke with a start. Euan was very quiet.

She hurried up the stairs to his room. She thought to herself that Euan had probably fallen asleep on the floor – he would often do that if he had been up early in the morning.

Eileen carefully pushed open the door in case he was behind it. At first she didn't see him amongst all the toys he was in a habit of spreading across his floor.

Then she saw he was slumped inside his toy chest with the lid resting on his slack shoulders. She yanked the lid up and grabbing Euan she saw that his face had a deathly bluish-white pallor. His body was very limp and she knew he was dead. She tried resuscitating him before calling 999.

Later in hospital doctors explained to Eileen that the weight of the lid crashing down on Euan had caused him to suffocate.

Toys

Each year millions of toys are sold in the UK. As a parent it is your responsibility to ensure the toys your child plays with are safely constructed and appropriate for his age group. Toys are meant to bring joy and fun but sadly they are frequently the cause of injury.

Reputable toy manufacturers sometimes miss dangers that are present in their toys despite rigorous testing; with almost every accident being unique in the way it happens, as children quite often do things that we do not expect them to do and they may find a way of doing something with a toy that the manufacturers never expected.

Many parents know how their child's mind operates. Look at his toys through his eyes. If he is in the habit of stripping the wheels and other parts off his toy cars, try and buy him more durable ones. In any event, particularly if there is a younger sibling in the house, once the wheels are off don't put them back on again. Put them away until the children are older and less likely to be destructive.

In the UK, toys that conform to safety standards will carry the CE mark on its label or packaging. Some will also have the Lion mark. Toys bearing these marks tell parents that the product does not contain dangerous chemicals, like lead, in paint; materials that can easily catch fire; any type of plug (only batteries or transformers are allowed) any small parts that a young child could choke on or any sharp edges.

Three-year-old Sammy had been given a toy tape player for his birthday by a family friend. It was one of those import types that greatly resembled the safer Fisher-Price and Little Tikes ones but which did not meet the same rigorous safety requirements of these reputable companies.

Sammy loved the idea of having his own machine that he could turn off and on and turn the tape over and not risk his parents wrath for playing with theirs.

One morning Sammy's mother, Judith, left her son playing in his room while she tidied up the house. But her house cleaning came to an abrupt halt when she was met by his tear-stained face.

Sammy stood in front of her clutching the tape recorder to his chest. Judith's first thought was that he had broken it and was bringing it to her to fix, but when she asked him what was wrong Sammy told her that his finger was stuck.

She led him over to the sofa and carefully sat him down while she examined the toy. Sure enough, his index finger was jammed under a small metal tab at the base of the tape-playing compartment.

Judith tried to gently pull his finger out but his screams put a halt to that. She also tried to break off the hinged door so she could prise the metal tab up to free her son's finger. The door wouldn't break easily and it was proving very painful for her son.

Judith bundled Sammy up carefully and drove him to the nearby Accident and Emergency department at a children's hospital.

Immediately, they were shown into a treatment room where a special team of trained nurses managed successfully to distract both Judith's and Sammy's attention while the hinged door was quickly snapped off and Sammy's finger released.

The nail bed of Sammy's index finger was very white and painful to the touch. After a drink of juice and some Calpol, Sammy was subsequently given an X-ray which revealed the tiny bone at the end of his finger had been crushed.

Judith was distraught that a child's toy could cause such an injury but it made a useful reminder that where children are concerned only toys that carry the CE mark or Lion mark are tested rigorously enough to withstand the demands of everyday use.

When choosing toys or games which are safe for older children remember that they may contain small parts which are hazardous in a younger child's hands. Your child could easily swallow tiny toys or there may be small, removable parts which can get stuck in your child's throat, ears or nose. Obviously, if you have younger children, you cannot ban your older child from the learning experience he will receive from playing with toys designed for his own age group. But take care that your younger child does not get his hands on them. If possible store these toys away from the younger child's toys.

As a rough guide do not let your child play with anything that is the same size or smaller than a 50-pence piece.

Pay particular attention to your child's age, interests and skill level when choosing toys. Appropriate selection should include quality design and construction. Make sure you understand all instructions and, if your child is old enough, make sure he understands how to operate or play the game too.

Fourteen-month-old Connel was always trying to keep up with his older sister. On one sunny spring afternoon, Connel's mum had let them out into the garden to play.

Connel watched enviously as his three-year-old sister raced around the patio on her tricycle. Though he had a small one, his sister's appeared much more fun.

As soon as Connel's sister had become bored with her trike and went off to play on the swings, Connel tried to climb onto it. It was far too big for him but he was determined. Eventually his mum lifted him on to it, his feet barely reached the concrete patio below, but he got enough grip with the tips of his toes to propel the bike.

His mum watched him for a bit as he teetered round the patio before going over to push her daughter on the swing. Suddenly there was a crash and Connel was crying. The trike, which he should never have been allowed to play on as it was far too big for him, had toppled over leaving Connel with a bad bruise on his head, grazed cheeks, hands and elbows and a chipped front tooth.

Immediately throw away all plastic wrappings on toys before they become deadly playthings. Never buy your child a toy without reading its labels first. If a manufacturer says on its label that the toy is 'not recommended for children under three', for example, do not buy that toy for an under-three. The recommendations are there for a reason, usually important safety ones. Look for other safety labels including: 'flame retardant/flame resistant' on fabric products and 'washable materials' on stuffed toys and dolls.

Always check your child's toys on a regular basis to make sure that none have become broken or come apart at the seams, exposing small parts or pellets that could be swallowed or inhaled. Watch out for stuffed toys which may have wires that could cut or stab. A damaged toy should be thrown away or repaired immediately. If a wooden toy has developed any rough surfaces these should be sanded smooth right away.

Furry toys are not a good idea for babies. If they decide to suck on the fur and get a mouthful of it they might choke.

Your child should be taught to put his toys away after play. This will prevent your child from falling on them and injuring himself.

If your child inherits older toys check them rigorously, especially for any parts that might break off and be swallowed by your child.

Do not buy young children toys that have long strings or cords. These cords could easily become wrapped around your child's neck.

Flying toys can injure eyes. Make sure your child understands this by teaching him never to point or fire a gun in somebody's face. If he is too young to understand, then he should not be allowed to play with such toys. Dart guns or arrows should have rubber suction cups or cork tips. Forbid your child to play with dart guns or other toys which could shoot things not intended for that gun, like pencils.

Do not allow a child to play with darts or any other adult sporting game that involves equipment with sharp points.

Do not allow very young children to play with balloons. Uninflated or broken balloons can choke or suffocate. More children have suffocated on uninflated balloons and pieces of broken balloons than on any other type of toy and, due to their natural desire to put everything in their mouths, young children under the age of three are at greater risk than older children from choking on toys. However, children aged three and older are more likely to choke on balloons.

Make sure any electric toys your child plays with are

sturdy and properly built to reduce the risk of shocks or burns. Teach older children how to play safely with them.

When buying a baby, or very young child, a rattle or other squeezy toy, make sure it's not small enough to fit inside your child's mouth.

The following checklist could also be used to check nursery equipment at a child-minder's home. Remember child-minders watch children to make money and some may have purchased very old equipment as a money-saver and they may not match up to safety regulations. It is important to check all equipment your child may come into contact with before employing a child-minder.

CHECKLIST

❑ Cradle has a sturdy bottom and a wide base for stability.

❑ Cradle has smooth surfaces, no protruding staples or hardware which may injure a baby.

❑ Legs have strong, effective locks to prevent folding while in use.

❑ Mattress is firm and fits snugly. If second-hand, check that it is not soiled or badly stained.

❑ Cot bars are spaced no more than two inches (five centimetres) apart.

❑ No cot bars are missing or cracked.

❑ Mattress fits snugly, less than two finger widths between edge of mattress and cot side.

❑ Mattress support is securely attached to the head and footboards.

❑ Corner posts are no higher than a sixteenth of an inch (one millimetre) to prevent entanglement of clothing or other objects worn by the child.

❑ No cut-outs in the head and footboards which allow head entrapment.

❑ Dropside catch cannot be easily released by baby.

❑ Dropside catches securely hold sides in raised position.

❑ All screws or bolts which secure components of crib are present and tight.

❑ Cot has a minimum rail height of 26 inches (66 centimetres).

❑ No strings or cords longer than seven inches (18 centimetres) should dangle in the cot.

❑ Cot gym should be removed from cot when a child can push up on hands and knees or reaches five months of age, whichever comes first.

❑ Toy parts are not small enough to be a choking hazard.

❑ Do not forget your baby's sleepwear. It should be well fitted and flame resistant. Blankets should also be fireproofed.

❑ When your child is 36-inches tall or is showing signs of being able to climb out of the cot, it is time to leave the cot and move into a bed.

❑ Use bumper pads with at least six ties so that they fit snugly against the entire perimeter of the cot, ties should be no longer than seven inches (18 centimetres) to avoid strangulation.

❑ When your child can stand in the cot, you need to remove the bumpers as these can be used to climb on to get out of the cot.

❑ When placing the cot in the nursery make sure that your child cannot reach lamps, electrical cords, shades or blinds, especially blind and shade cords.

❑ Do not place the crib near a window, especially on the second level of a house.

❑ Do not leave rattles, teethers or toys in the crib. They can become wedged in a baby's mouth causing suffocation.

❑ Never leave your child unattended on top of a changing table.

❑ Never put baby-bouncer seats on top of a table or kitchen worktop.

❑ Never use a bouncer seat as a car seat.

❑ Never leave your child unattended in an infant swing.

❑ Never leave your child unattended in a baby-walker and use on smooth, flat surfaces only.

❑ Do not use walkers anywhere near stairs that do not have a gate.

❑ Never tie a toy across the top of a playpen or cot.

❑ When selecting toys, consider the child's age, interests

and skill level; look for quality design and construction; and follow age and safety recommendations on labels. Remember: if there are older children in the house, younger siblings are at risk.

❑ Tie up or cut off all curtain or blind cords.

❑ Teach children to put toys away safely after play.

❑ Ensure toys intended for younger children are stored separately from those for older children.

❑ Inspect old and new toys regularly for damage and potential hazards. Make any necessary repairs immediately or throw damaged toys away.

❑ Remove all crib toys which are strung across the cot or playpen when your child is beginning to push up on his hands and knees or is five months old, whichever happens first.

❑ Ensure all toy chests have lid-support devices which will ensure the lid does not unexpectedly fall on your child.

❑ Children have suffocated when plastic bags have blocked the nose and mouth and prevented breathing – do not let your child have access to these.

❑ Do not allow children under the age of six to play with uninflated balloons without supervision. Immediately collect the pieces of broken balloons and dispose of them out of the reach of children.

❏ Keep small balls and other smooth round objects away from babies and children who have a tendency to put things in their mouths.

❏ Regularly check the batteries in your baby-listener.

❏ Never tie your baby's dummy around his neck.

❏ Babies can roll off changing tables from a very young age – never leave them alone.

CHAPTER SEVEN

GARDEN AND GARAGE

Like the rest of your house, your garden and garage needs to be baby-proofed just as thoroughly. Children love to play outside as everything is a potential adventure waiting to be explored.

GARDEN

Never let your toddler play alone outside. He is not old enough to tell right from wrong and will not know how to extricate himself from a dangerous situation. Chasing and catching a bee is a good game to a youngster who does not know any better. Even a baby napping in a pram should not be left without almost constant supervision.

It's also a good idea not to let your child play in your front garden unless it is completely fenced in. Children can dart between parked cars and if they dash out from between them into the path of an oncoming vehicle they could be seriously injured.

Youngsters also do not know how unsafe it is to hide

under parked cars. If someone was to drive off while the child was underneath, he might be crushed.

PADDLING-POOLS, PONDS AND OTHER WATER GARDENS

Children should always be constantly supervised when playing in a paddling-pool. Remember to empty the pool immediately after every use and never leave it with any water in it. An inch is all it takes for a child to drown.

Garden ponds and other types of water gardens are equally dangerous. Water is among the first places a child will make a beeline for. Ideally, garden ponds should be filled in and made into sandpits until the child is older. If this is not an option, cover it with fine, sturdy, wire mesh like chicken wire or an iron grille making sure that it won't collapse if your child climbs on it. Other types of water gardens should also be drained and filled in with plants until children are much older.

Three-year-old Jane was playing in the enclosed back garden with her chums Tommy and John while her mum, Vicky, had a coffee with her friends' mother in the kitchen.

The two mums could hear the children's voices from where they sat and knew they were all right on their own. After a while, Vicky realised she could no longer hear Jane's voice and went into the garden. Tommy and John were busy playing with their cars but there was no sign of Jane.

The four-year-old twins did not know where Jane had gone. Vicky quickly looked around the garden and with her heart pounding saw that the garden gate was open. She ran out into the street, calling Jane's name: but there was no response. Her friend Josie joined her. They looked in the road and the front gardens of the neighbouring houses before Vicky started looking in the back gardens.

The house next to Josie's did not have a garden fence. It was the home of a retired couple who were away on holiday.

Vicky ran into the back garden. After calling Jane's name several times she was about to move on to another house when she suddenly saw her child's shoe sticking up from the murky depths of a large garden pond.

Vicky pulled her daughter out and tried resuscitating her while Josie dialled 999.

The paramedics reached Jane virtually within minutes of being called, but Jane had not drawn breath for almost 15 minutes. She was rushed to hospital where doctors managed to resuscitate the child. A feat they said they were only able to do probably because it was winter and the water was extremely cold.

Jane miraculously survived after being clinically dead for 40 minutes but as a result she is now severely brain damaged.

It is not enough to let your child outside and assume the garden gate is shut and locked. A vigilant parent should always double-check it, making sure at the same time that there isn't anything nearby a child could climb onto to open the gate. A young child should never be left unsupervised inside or outside a home.

DROWNING

When a child drowns it usually happens quickly, silently and, typically, when a child has been left unattended or during a brief lapse of supervision.

A child will lose consciousness within two minutes of being under water. If he is discovered within the first couple of minutes he has a much greater chance of survival. After four to six minutes irreversible brain damage occurs. Depending on the length of time a child has been submerged, most near-drownings carry a risk of neurological damage. Nearly all who require cardiopulmonary resuscitation (CPR) either die or are left with brain damage.

Never let your young child out of your sight, particularly if water is nearby.

Two-year-old Sam loved to race around the garden with his older sister's friends. Sometimes they told him to go away, that he was a baby and not old enough to play with them.

This particular afternoon the children were bursting to go into the garden. It had been raining for days and they had not been allowed outside. Finally the sun was shining. A group of five-year-old Georgina's playmates came to join her in her large back garden. The older children shouted and laughed as they played.

Georgina left her friends momentarily to ask her mum if she and her friends could have some juice. As she ran back to the house she spotted Sam. To her it looked like he was standing on his head inside a small dustbin at the side of the house. She shouted for her mum because Sam wouldn't come out when she asked what he was doing.

Tragically, Sam was dead. He drowned in the few inches of rainwater that had collected in the bin as it lay outside.

Young children's heads are heavier than the rest of their bodies making them top-heavy. In tragic cases like Sam's he was unable to pull himself out because of the weight imbalance.

GENERAL GARDEN MAINTENANCE

Check the childrens' play area frequently, watching out for broken paving stones which need repairing or to be cleared of mud or moss which can be very slippery when wet. Also look for loose boards on fences, steps, sheds and garages and holes in the lawn that need to be filled in.

Make sure you keep play areas clean of all animal droppings.

If you have a washing-line or rotary drier in the garden, ensure the lines are kept high up. Children have been strangled on lines that have been allowed to dangle down.

Make sure your garden is properly fenced if you are to allow a child to play outside. Make sure the gate is always kept locked and do not leave anything next to the gate or fence that encourages a child to escape.

If your youngster is at an age where he still puts things in his mouth make sure that stones, twigs and dirt are not used as an alternative to teethers and dummies.

Garden bonfires should be kept well away from trees, hedges, fences and sheds as well as your house. Your bonfire should only contain small, manageable pieces of branches and be kept small enough so that it does not burn out of control. Like water, children have a fascination for fire so make sure your child is kept at a safe distance from the bonfire and under an adult's supervision.

Teach your baby about dangers he may find in the garden, like rose bushes and other thorny or poisonous plants. Teach your child to respect bees and wasps. Use the created vocabulary of 'Ouch!' or 'Sharp!' as in the home.

Tidy up after every gardening job. Clutter and debris not only looks untidy it causes accidents

A broken fence or open gate is considered as an open invitation to play in traffic. Check fences and gates regularly to make sure that they are shut and locked and in good condition.

Do not leave a hose lying loose. Your child could trip over it or use it for something that might result in another accident.

Keep children away from barbecues at all times, especially when you are cooking.

LAWNMOWERS AND OTHER GARDEN TOOLS

Keep your child out of the area altogether when outdoor power equipment is being used or the lawn is being mowed. Flying debris can seriously injure a small child. Never allow a child to ride or operate a garden mower, even if the child is supervised.

Keep children indoors and supervised. Never assume your child will remain where you last saw him.

Be alert and turn off the mower if your child enters the mowing area and use extra care when backing up or when approaching corners, shrubs or trees.

Always switch off and unplug electrical tools if they are to be unattended, even for a moment.

Teenagers should only be allowed to operate outdoor power tools and equipment if they possess adequate strength and maturity to do so safely.

PLAY EQUIPMENT

Hundreds of children are injured each year in falls from outdoor play equipment.

Teach your child how to use a slide or the swings safely and lend a supporting hand until they develop the skills and confidence to do it by themselves.

Make sure they know not to walk behind moving swings or other equipment that is in use and to hold on tightly when on a climbing frame.

Make sure the play equipment you choose for your child matches his age and capability. For example, toddlers should have small slides and swings designed so they cannot fall off.

YOUR CHILD'S PLAY AREA

Hard surface areas should be avoided, like asphalt or concrete. If you site your child's play equipment on the grass, make sure it is well watered. Dried-out soil can be very hard.

Ideally, the ground area around this equipment should help absorb the impact of a child's fall. Some good examples are loose-fill materials such as soft woodchips, pea gravel, fine sand, rubber matting and shredded rubber. These materials should be maintained at a minimum depth of 9–12 inches (23–30 centimetres) and should extend a minimum of 72 inches (180 centimetres) in all directions around stationary equipment. If very young children are to use this play area, make sure they do not put any of the surfacing materials in their mouths as they could choke.

Provide lots of room between play equipment and other solid features such as a fence or the garage, to allow your child to run around or fall without hurting himself. Pay particular attention to moving equipment such as swings and seesaws.

Ensure there are no sharp points or edges, nuts or bolts sticking out on equipment; narrow gaps in metal connections or open 'S' hooks at the top and bottom of swings which could all harm your child.

Elevated surfaces such as platforms, ramps and bridgeways should have guard rails to prevent falls. But make sure that any openings in the guard rails and the spaces between the platforms and between ladder rungs measure less than three and a half inches (eight centimetres) or more than nine inches (23 centimetres). Children can get trapped and strangle in openings where they can fit their bodies but not their heads through the space.

Suspension bridges, roundabouts or seesaws, should not have accessible moving parts that might crush or pinch a child's fingers.

Check there are not any raised concrete edges, sudden changes in surface elevation, or raised tree roots, stumps or rocks which could trip your child.

Make a regular check of your child's play area to make sure it's in good condition. Immediately replace missing, broken or worn out components; tighten up any loose nuts or bolts; check for deterioration in wood, metal or plastic materials and repair or replace; maintain the proper 12-inch depth of surfacing material around the play area and clean up any debris.

PLANTS

Check the suitability of all plants in your garden. Every year thousands of people, the majority under seven years old, are poisoned by touching or eating plants. Children cannot resist putting things in their mouths. Be particularly wary about berries and fungi that you suspect might be poisonous or a choking hazard. Before buying new plants check whether they are poisonous or liable to cause allergies, including skin irritation, if touched or brushed against.

A reputable garden nursery should be able to identify any plants or trees in your garden that you are unsure of. Take a cutting including a good length of stem, leaves and any flowers or berries that it produces.

A few plants which are commonly found in British gardens and are highly poisonous are: deadly nightshade (its shiny purple berries might be very tempting); woody nightshade (bright red berries) and foxgloves.

Thorny plants are another type you may want to consider removing. Some thorns can grow several inches long and could prove lethal to a child's eyesight should he stumble into the bush.

Keep an eye out for mushrooms or toadstools in the garden and pull them out as soon as they appear.
Remember young children will eat anything, and that includes plants.

Darren was playing in the garden when his mum called him into the house to get ready for dinner. He looked pale when he came in and she thought he was probably tired. He had been up very early that morning.

While the seven-year-old was upstairs in the

bathroom washing his hands she heard him vomiting and start to cry.

She ran upstairs and saw what looked like bits of chewed-up leaves in the toilet and asked him if he had eaten anything while he was playing in the garden. Darren, thinking he was now in trouble, cried a bit longer before admitting that he had.

Shirley called the hospital's Accident and Emergency department who told her to bring her son in so doctors could check him out. They also asked if she knew which plant her son had eaten. Shirley eventually managed to get Darren to show her the plant and she took cuttings of its leaves and stem as the nurse had asked her to.

Fortunately for Darren it was one that would not cause any lasting harm. Shirley learned from the nurses that children were easily poisoned from eating plants, and although most would only cause some vomiting and diarrhoea others such as Deadly Nightshade or Laburnum which are commonly found in gardens could be fatal.

The next day Shirley took cuttings of the leaves and stems of all the plants in her garden to a reputable garden centre to have them identified. She did not want to risk her son's health again.

SUN PROTECTION FOR CHILDREN

Children love playing outside on warm sunny days, but too much sun can be dangerous. Every year thousands of children visit hospital as a result of being sunburnt. Over-exposure to the sun's ultra-violet rays not only causes painful sunburn, but can lead to life-threatening skin cancer in later life.

Teach your child from a young age good sun sense. Apply sunscreen liberally – remembering backs and tops of ears, tops of feet and behind the neck and knees – before your child goes out and reapply every two hours if your child has been swimming, even waterproof sunscreens can come off. A sunscreen with Sun Protection Factor (SPF) of at least 15 will block most harmful ultraviolet rays. Children under six months of age should never have sunscreen applied to their skin, but should be protected by avoiding sun exposure entirely.

The sun's rays are strongest between 11 a.m. and 3 p.m. so limit your child's exposure to the sun during these hours.

Make sure your child wears a hat with a wide brim which offers good protection to eyes, ears, face and the back of the neck.

Dress your child in loose-fitting clothes with a tight-weave material to keep the sun from penetrating through the cloth and burning young skin.

In Australia, children have been taught good sun practices through an effective advertising campaign – *Slip–Slap–Slop*: slip on a T-shirt, slap on a hat, slop on some sunscreen.

It's a campaign that should be adopted by parents throughout the UK.

GARAGES AND SHEDS
A garage or shed can be an exciting place of exploration for a young child. The multitude of tools, pots and other equipment he sees Daddy or Mummy 'playing with' can prove an irresistable temptation. Keep doors locked at all times and keep the key well out of reach of young children. Even if you are pottering in your garden and

therefore in and out of the garage and shed frequently, keep it locked. It only takes a moment for your back to be turned for an accident to happen.

Four-year-old Stanley went into the garden shed while his dad was cutting the grass. His dad had a large workbench which he would spend hours at a time fixing things or making things. Stanley was in awe of his dad and was desperate to make something himself, even though his dad had forbidden him from touching his tools. Stanley decided that he would surprise his dad; he would show him how grown-up he was by making him something that he would be proud of.

Stanley climbed up onto the workbench and reached for the heavy metal toolbox which his dad stored on a shelf above. It was far too heavy for the boy but he was determined to lift it. He had just managed to grasp the toolbox's handle and started to pull it down when the box fell over, spraying a range of sharp implements over Stanley's head.

Stanley barely survived. He's now blind in one eye and has numerous scars to serve as a reminder of his escapade.

Many things in your garage or shed are not only dangerous but lethal. Death can occur when a child swallows such everyday substances as barbecue-lighter fluid, paint thinner or antifreeze.

Ensure all poisons have child-resistant caps or lids and that they are stored in their original containers. Never decant them into soft-drink bottles or anything else that may be mistaken for the original contents of a food or drink container.

Some poisons, such as fertilisers, come in boxes that could be easily accessed by curious fingers. Either store these items on a high shelf well out of reach of children in a shed or garage that is locked at all times. Or, put them in a locking container with the key kept in a place where your child cannot get it.

GREENHOUSES

Greenhouses can be particularly dangerous if you store any weedkillers, fertilisers or pesticides inside. Keep it locked at all times if you do. If that's not possible, store these items in a locked strongbox or secured away in the garage.

If you have a greenhouse, consider taking it down if it's in a spot that is likely to interfere with children's play. If that is not feasible, cover the glass at the bottom with special safety film or board it up round the bottom.

And do not forget about cold frames. They contain glass too and are often placed in vulnerable positions for children.

> Friends Sean and Steven were football mad. Whenever the two boys were together, you could be sure they were either kicking a ball or talking about the sport.
>
> One Saturday afternoon, the pair were in Sean's back garden. His dad had just warned them, as he always did when they played out back, to keep the ball away from the house and the greenhouse.

There would be trouble, he would say, if any of his greenhouse glass or the house windows were broken.

The boys were impersonating their favourite players, recreating goals they had scored.

Typically for 11-year-old boys, they forgot Sean's dad's warning about keeping away from the greenhouse, concentrating solely on the game at hand. It was during one of their more robust tackles that the boys found themselves falling straight through the greenhouse door.

Hearing the breaking glass, Sean's dad ran out to find both boys lying in a pool of shattered glass and blood.

Later in hospital, the boys lacerations to their arms, abdomens and head – some of which were quite deep – were stitched up and doctors told them how lucky they had been to escape severe injury. The week before one had tried to save the life of a little boy who had been running on a patio, tripped and fell through the sliding glass doors. The little boy had died.

DRIVEWAYS

It is a sad fact of life that every year children are crushed to death by cars reversing while playing in their own driveways. Always know where your child is and if you or someone else is reversing from your drive always keep your children in sight. Do not let your child race out to say hello to Daddy or Granny as they pull into the drive. As with any accident it is needless, but this is one which is particularly sad as it often involves another family member or close friend.

COMMUNAL GARDENS

Before letting your child out to play in a communal garden, check it out and maintain it as if it were your own. After all, it is your child's safety.

CHECKLIST

❏ Never leave a young child to play unsupervised in your garden.

❏ Always supervise a child while playing in or near water.

❏ Empty your child's paddling-pool immediately after use.

❏ Garden ponds and other water gardens should be drained and filled in.

❏ Keep your garden in good order.

❏ Do not allow your child in the garden while a lawnmower is in use.

❏ Power tools should be used and stored away from children.

❏ Maintain your child's play area and equipment.

❏ Rid your garden of poisonous plants and those with long thorns.

❏ Never let your child play in the sun without adequate sunscreen and clothes to avoid burning and over-exposure.

❏ Keep garages and sheds locked at all times.

❑ Never decant poisonous substances into old food or drink containers.

❑ Keep all hazardous substances out of your child's reach.

❑ Your child should not be allowed to play on the driveway – always watch for children while reversing your car.

❑ Dismantle your greenhouse or board up the lower level of glass.

❑ If your children play in a communal garden, make sure it's safe.

CHAPTER EIGHT

EMERGENCY ACTION

One of the most important things about dealing with an emergency is to keep calm. Of course, that's easier said than done when it's your child who is injured. A first-aid course is always a good thing to have taken, and it just might help you cope when emergency action is required.

GIVING CHILDREN MEDICINE

A little imagination never hurts when it comes to giving your child medicine, but be very careful not to describe medicine as sweeties. Children have a habit of searching out these 'sweeties' when a parent's back is turned.

Make sure you give your child the right dose at the right time. Incorrect dosage can be dangerous whether its over-the-counter (OTC) medicine or prescription drugs. Before giving your child any medication read instructions or the prescription label carefully. There are many warnings and they are written for a reason.

Make sure the product is safe for your child's age group. If there is no mention of dosage for children under

12, do not assume it is safe. Overdosing can also occur if a child is given more than one medicine with similar ingredients. Always check with your GP or chemist before giving your child more than one type of medicine to ensure there are no risks.

Always use proper medicinal dosage spoons, cups or syringes when giving your child medication and never use an ordinary teaspoon as one type of teaspoon may be twice the size of another.

If in any doubt about dosage or giving your child any medicine teletelephone your GP or chemist immediately.

The following are a list of questions a parent should ask before giving a child any medication:
• If your child is on other medication, ask if this new one will be compatible with it.
• How often and for how long does my child need to take it?
• What if my child misses a dose?
• Are there side effects and if so what are they?
• Do not give your child any OTC medication if the safety-seal appears to have been tampered with or broken.

If you are not happy with the way your child reacts to a drug do not assume that everything is all right. It is better to make the extra calls to your GP than to have your child suffer a bad drug reaction.

CHOKING, SUFFOCATION AND STRANGULATION
Choking, suffocation and strangulation are a huge risk

for young children in everyday life. A child will choke if his airway becomes blocked by food or an object; he will suffocate if his nose and mouth become covered and he will strangle if something becomes tightly wrapped around his neck.

Children, especially babies, will put anything in their mouths. It is up to you to protect them by keeping dangerous items out of their reach and by avoiding certain foods which commonly cause children to choke. Balloons and coins, especially pennies, are the most common cause of choking among children.

Remove hood and neck drawstrings from all clothing. In the UK, they are outlawed from being incorporated in children's clothing. Throw away any old sewing patterns that include hood or neck drawstrings. Never allow children to wear necklaces, handbags, scarves or clothing with drawstrings on play equipment. All too often these items get caught up on something and strangle a child.

Always supervise small children while eating and playing.

Be careful when giving children the following foods:
- Sausages and hot dogs.
- Peanuts, sunflower seed and other nuts.
- Hard sweets and mints.
- Popcorn.
- Grapes.
- Raisins.
- Raw carrot.
- Seeds and pips in fruit.
- Bones in fish, meat and poultry.

Keep the following items away from your young child:

- Small parts to toys.
- Deflated balloons or pieces of balloons that have burst.
- Jewellery.
- Buttons.
- Small batteries for watches, calculators and other small electronic devices.
- Marbles, jacks and small plastic building bricks.
- Safety pins (make sure you do not put them within reach of a child when changing nappies).
- Nails, tacks, drawing pins, screws.
- Sewing items, such as needles and pins.
- Coins.
- Eyes and noses that can be torn from dolls and stuffed animals.
- Broken crayons.
- Cocktail sticks.
- Hair accessories, such as hair grips and slides.
- Beer caps.

You can protect your child from choking by taking the following steps:

- Cut food into small pieces before giving it to a child.
- Never allow children to run with food in their mouths.
- Do not allow children to lie down while eating.
- Check dummies to make sure the teat cannot be pulled loose.
- Do not allow your child to drink from a polystyrene cup. Small pieces can be bitten or broken off and cause your child to choke if swallowed.
- Check the floors and tables often to make sure you

have not left jewellery, loose change or other items within your child's reach.
- Check toys to make sure that have not been broken or that parts are not coming loose.
- Keep purses, jewellery boxes and tool boxes out of reach.
- Do not give your child latex balloons.
- Make sure baby-sitters and child-minders know about the dangers of choking.

WHAT TO DO IF YOUR CHILD STARTS CHOKING:

If the child can still cough forcefully then he is still getting some air. Encourage the child to cough while you dial 999.

If a child or baby can only cough weakly or cannot make any sound at all emergency action is needed:

For a baby under one year old
1) Give five sharp slaps on the back between the shoulder blades.
2) Turn the baby over onto your lap, supporting his head with one hand and put two or three fingers in the centre of the breastbone just below the nipples and push down on the chest five times about a half- to one-inch deep.
3) Repeat the back slaps then another five chest pushes. Continue until the baby starts to breathe. However, if it loses consciousness take the steps described below:

If the baby loses consciousness
1) Place the baby on a hard, flat surface.
2) Open the baby's mouth and if you see an object sweep

it out. Be careful not to push the object further down the baby's throat.

3) Open the baby's airway and give two slow breaths. If they do not go in, reposition the head and try to give breaths again. (Be gentle. If you blow too hard you will damage the baby's lungs.)

4) If the air still does not go in, give five back slaps and five chest pushes.

5) Check for an object and sweep it out if possible.

6) If the baby still does not breathe or regain consciousness dial 999 immediately and continue to repeat the above steps until help arrives.

For a child aged between one and eight years old use the Heimlich manoeuvre

1) Wrap your arms around the child from behind.

2) Place the thumb side of your fist against the abdomen just above the navel. Grasp the fist with your other hand.

3) Give quick upward thrusts. Repeat until the child can breathe.

If the child becomes unconscious

1) Lay the child on his back.

2) Look in the mouth. If you see an object sweep it out. Be careful not to push the object further down the throat.

3) Give two slow breaths. If the breaths do not go in, reposition the head and try to give breaths again.

4) If the air still does not go in, with the heel of one hand give five quick, upward abdominal thrusts.

5) If the child still does not breathe dial 999 immediately and continue repeating the above steps until help arrives.

SUFFOCATION

If your child is suffocating because his air passages are blocked, remove the obstruction. If the child is not breathing, begin resuscitation.

STRANGULATION

This happens when something is wound tightly round your child's neck. Unwind the item, and if the child is not breathing, begin resuscitation.

POISONING

Children are more likely than adults to suffer more seriously or die from poisoning due to their size, faster metabolic rates and because their bodies cannot deal with toxic chemicals. Children are also more likely to be poisoned because of their habit of putting everything in their mouths.

Many parents know to keep medications locked away from their child, but it's important to know too that the majority of poisonings are from non-pharmaceutical products such as household cleaners, plants, alcohol, cosmetics and insect killers.

The number of deaths through poisoning has declined due largely to child-resistant packing, product reformulations, heightened parental awareness and appropriate intervention by health care officials.

Below are some general precautions that can lower the chances for mishaps involving poison.

Keep all medicines and hazardous products locked up and out of reach when not in use. When choosing child care facilities or when visiting other homes make sure poisons are not within reach. Do not rely completely on close supervision for prevention, because many accidents happen to children while parents or carers are nearby.

Since the introduction of child-resistant containers the numbers of poisonings have dramatically decreased. Make sure you always ask for child-resistant containers for all medications and household cleaners. Remember a child-resistant cap does not stop a child from opening a lid, it only slows him down.

Do not take medicine in front of a young child. A child might wrongly believe they are sweets and go in search of them as soon as your back is turned. Or he may take the medication during a game of pretending to be Mum or Dad or another grown-up.

Make sure young children have access to safe snacks in a ground-level cupboard so they will not be tempted to try poisonous substances.

Flush unused medications down the toilet. Do not stockpile them.

If you are called away while using something like bleach or any other poisonous substance, take it with you. Do not allow your child to take part in chores such as painting, paint removal, floor stripping and pesticide or fertiliser use.

Never decant hazardous substances into food or drink containers. Children and adults alike are poisoned every year by drinking or eating from a container whose original contents had been replaced by a poisonous substance.

Do not mix chemicals! Always read the labels. Even common household cleaners can emit toxic gases when mixed together. When using toxic products wear protective clothing and work in ventilated areas and do not allow your child in the same room.

Many household products are brightly coloured and

packaged attractively. Remember that children under the age of five cannot read labels and curious young children put almost anything in their hands into their mouths. Strong smells do not stop children from tasting things such as bleach, petrol and lighter fluid.

If your child swallows any kind of poison or medication:
1) Call 999 immediately. Bring the container, if there is one, to the telephone with you. Try to identify the substance your child has swallowed to the emergency operator.
2) Do not give your child anything to eat or drink. Wet his lips if they are burning.
3) Do not give your child salt water or anything else to make him vomit unless the emergency operator tells you to do so.

WHAT TO DO IF YOUR CHILD STOPS BREATHING
A child can stop breathing for a number of reasons, for example if he has been submerged under water. When breathing stops, this lack of vital oxygen will soon stop your child's heart and will affect the brain.

If your child stops breathing but still has a pulse:
1) Get someone to call 999 immediately. If you are alone give about one minute of rescue breathing before calling 999.
2) Tilt your child's head back and lift his chin. This pulls the tongue up and opens your child's airway. Check for breathing when the head is in this position.
3) If your child is still not breathing, keep the airway

open, pinch your child's nose shut, open your mouth wide and make a tight seal around your child's mouth, or nose and mouth if it is still a baby.

4) Give two slow breaths and watch for the chest rising.

5) Check your child's pulse at the groove in his neck next to his windpipe (in a baby check for a pulse on the inside of your baby's upper arm), for five to ten seconds.

6) Repeat one slow breath about every three seconds until your child starts to breathe on his own.

7) Check the pulse again after the first minute and then every few minutes. If your child loses his pulse, start giving him CPR (cardiopulmonary resuscitation).

If your child stops breathing and has no pulse:

1) Start Baby CPR – aged one and under (see below).

2) Send someone to dial 999 immediately. If you are by yourself give CPR for one minute then call 999.

3) Open the baby's airway and give two slow breaths.

4) Check for a pulse on the inside of the arm between the elbow and the shoulder.

If there is no pulse, give chest compressions (Baby CPR):

1) Place two fingers on the centre of the breastbone just below the nipples.

2) Push straight down on the chest five times in three seconds.

3) Tilt your baby's head back, cover his mouth and nose with your mouth, and give one slow breath.

4) Check your baby's pulse and breathing. If there is no pulse continue sets of five compressions and one breath until help arrives.

Child CPR – aged one to eight
1) Send someone to dial 999 immediately. If you are by yourself give CPR for one minute then call 999.
2) Open the airway, cover your child's mouth with your own and give two slow breaths and watch for the chest to rise.
3) Place one hand in the centre of the chest over the breastbone.
4) Position your shoulders over your hand. Compress the chest five times in about three seconds. Give one slow breath.
5) Check your child's pulse and breathing. If the child has no pulse, continue sets of five compressions and one breath until help arrives.

BURNS AND SCALDS
Burns can be extremely painful, no matter how small. However, the level of pain is not necessarily related to the severity of the burn – some of the worst burns can be relatively painless. If in any doubt immediately call your GP, your local hospital emergency department or dial 999. Always dial 999 for major or serious-looking burns.

For minor burns apply the following tips:
- If the skin is unbroken, run cool water over the area of the burn or soak it in cool water (not ice water), keeping the area submerged for at least ten minutes. Taking the heat out of a burn will stop it damaging the skin any further. A clean, cold compress or wet towel will help reduce pain.
- If the burn is in a place where it can not easily be flushed with cool running water, wrap a bag of frozen

peas or other frozen vegetable in a damp tea-towel and apply to the burned area. Never apply ice or other similar products directly onto a burn. Always wrap it in a damp cloth first.

- Remove any tight jewellery or belts if they are near the affected area as burns can make the skin swell up.
- Reassure and comfort the child. Burns can be extremely painful
- After flushing or soaking, cover the burn with a sterile bandage (if available) or clean cloth if it's in an area where the blistered area might get bumped or rubbed. Protect the burn from pressure or friction and do not break any blisters.
- Minor burns will generally heal without additional treatment.

Dial 999 or hospital emergency room if:
1) You are unsure how severe the burn is.
2) The burn covers more than one area of the body or one large area.
3) The child has difficulty in breathing.

Burns caused by electricity
1) Turn off the power before you touch your child.
2) Check to make sure your child is breathing and has a pulse. If he is not breathing start resuscitation.
3) Cover any burns with a dry, clean cloth.
4) Call your GP or dial 999 depending on how serious it is.

Burns caused by chemicals:
1) Flush the area with large amounts of cool water.

2) Call your GP or dial 999 for advice on medical attention.

EYES
If your child has some grit or an eyelash in his eye, remove it very carefully. Ask your child not to rub his eye. If you cannot remove the item, or cannot see what it is, take your child to hospital.

If something has splashed into your child's eye, place his head backwards under a tap and flush the eye with cold water for ten minutes before going to hospital.

IF YOUR CHILD PUTS SOMETHING UP HIS NOSE OR IN HIS EAR
Always enlist the help of a doctor to retrieve any item your child might have shoved up his nose or stuffed down his ear.

MINOR INJURIES
If your child has a minor cut, press on it to stop the bleeding. If it's dirty, wash the wound in warm, soapy water. If necessary, apply a small dressing or plaster.

INSECT STINGS
If the insect has left its stinger behind, gently remove it with the help of tweezers. Calamine or Caladryl lotion will help soothe the sting and a paste of bicarbonate of soda and water will help bee stings while a paste of baking powder and water will help wasp stings.

If your child's sting starts to swell up fast or they have

been stung in the mouth, call an ambulance right away.

ROAD ACCIDENTS

If your child is hit by a car check to see whether he is conscious, that he is breathing and has a pulse or if he is bleeding severely.

Do not move your child unless absolutely necessary.

Keep your child still and support his head in line with his body.

Call 999 or get someone else to do it for you.

If your child is not breathing, open the airway and do rescue breathing, and if your child has no pulse, give CPR.

Use direct pressure on a wound that is bleeding severely.

Cover your child with a blanket, if necessary, to stop him from becoming chilled.

FALLS

If your child has a nasty fall make sure he is conscious, that he is breathing and has a pulse. Look for any severe bleeding or signs of head, neck or back injury.

If your child has fallen more than half to one metre in height, do not move him unless absolutely necessary. and call 999 immediately.

If your child is in pain and his shoulder, arm or leg is bruised and swollen, support the injured part with a pillow, folded blanket or towel to stop it from moving and wrap an icepack, or bag of frozen peas, in a cloth and put it on the injured part to reduce pain and swelling.

Make the child as comfortable as possible without moving the injured part and call your GP for medical advice.

How to Control Bleeding

If your child has an open wound immediately try to stop the bleeding. In most cases you can control bleeding with direct pressure by putting a dressing (gauze pads or a folded clean cloth) over the wound and pressing directly on the wound with your hand. Raise the area if possible by laying your child down and elevating his legs and maintain pressure by wrapping a bandage snugly over the dressing.

If the bleeding continues maintain direct pressure and dial 999.

Reassure your child and keep him comfortable. Do not let your child become chilled or overheated.

First-Aid Kit

Every household should have some type of first-aid kit, and if you do not already have one, assemble some supplies now. Tailor the contents to fit your family's particular needs. Do not add first-aid supplies to the jumble of toothpaste and cosmetics in the medicine cabinet.

Assemble them in a suitable, labelled box, such as a fishing-tackle box or a small tool chest with a hinged cover, so that everything will be handy when needed. Make sure everything has clear labels explaining what types of injuries they are to be used for.

Be sure not to lock the box, otherwise you may be hunting for the key when the emergency occurs. Place the box on a shelf beyond the reach of small children and check it periodically. Always restock items as soon as they are used up.

Keep all medications, including non-prescription drugs such as aspirin and paracetamol, in a separate locked box and out of reach of children.

Here is a list of suggested items for your first-aid box:
- bandages or surgical tape.
- sterile gauze packs – various sizes.
- absorbent cotton.
- adhesive tape.
- tweezers.
- sharp scissors.
- cotton-tipped swabs.
- tissues.
- thermometer.
- first-aid manual.
- antiseptic solution and cream.
- plasters.
- antihistamine cream such as Caladryl for insect bites and stings and Calamine lotion.
- ice pack.
- needle for splinter removal.

CHAPTER NINE

OUT AND ABOUT

The first time you let your child go somewhere alone will be a major milestone for both you and him. Naturally, you will worry yourself sick until his safe return and you will probably bug the life out of him by asking endless questions.

A parent cannot be with their child every moment of every day. The best thing you can do for him is to teach him how to stand on his own two feet, how to use his own common sense and not to be led on by others. By doing this you are helping to equip your child for life.

Of course, teaching him how to keep himself safe from harm, to ask himself if what he is about to do will pose any risk of injury, will also give him a good start in life.

TRAFFIC SENSE
Teaching your child about traffic is very important. Road accidents are the biggest single cause of accidental

death for children aged 14 years and younger. In 1996, 211 children were killed and more than 40,000 were injured.

The government and other organisations campaign endlessly for drivers to reduce their speeds in areas where children are present. A child hit by a car driving at 20 mph will probably sustain minor injuries; at 30 mph a child will be seriously injured and may die; at 40 mph the child will more than likely die from his injuries.

Experts believe that a child from the age of three is old enough to begin learning proper road safety. Most local authorities operate traffic clubs, sending children between the ages of three and five educational packs every six months.

From the age of three a child can be taught to stay on the pavement and that roads are dangerous. As your child gets older he can be taught how to cross a road safely. Obviously, young children could probably tell you in theory where they should cross a road and what to look out for. But, in practice, youngsters usually forget if they are in a hurry or excited. Even a 13-year-old will make mistakes.

It also pays to be very direct with your child about road safety. Telling your child he might get hurt if he runs into the road without looking is not enough. Tell him he will be killed, that he will never see his mummy or daddy again. It's that serious.

Every time you go out with your child, discuss how they should cross the road; how they should never walk out from between parked cars as drivers may not see them; that they should use pedestrian crossings wherever possible and teach your child how to use them.

Practise what you preach, even if you are in a hurry. Every time you cross the road point out that your child should always stand at the side of the road, looking and listening for traffic, waiting for a safe opportunity to cross.

BIKE SAFETY

Bicycles are associated with more childhood injuries than any other consumer product except the car.

Make sure your child wears bright clothing when cycling and never allow your child out without adequate reflective material on both himself and the bike.

Always buy a bike that will fit your child today not one he will grow into later. When choosing a bike for your child take into account his experience and ability. Make sure he can easily use both hand and foot brakes without falling over or jamming

Rubber-coated or metal pedals with serrated edges are far better than plastic ones which could be slippery. Firmly attached toeclips will also help stop your child's feet from slipping off the pedals.

Young children should not ride in the road as they do not have the skills to identify and avoid dangerous traffic situations.

Older children like to tinker with their bikes. Explain the risks of losing or seriously injuring a finger, especially the risk to younger siblings whose curiosity to touch overrides the danger factor, when spinning bicycle wheels or the bike's chain.

Help reduce your child's likelihood of losing control and having an accident by spelling out the dangers of:
- Riding in wet conditions which makes braking difficult.
- Riding a bike that is too big.

- Riding too fast.
- Riding double.
- Doing stunts.
- Striking a hole, bump or other object.
- Riding on grass or other wet, slippery surfaces.

Teach you child some common-sense rules when riding his bike:
- Make sure your child knows the rules of the road before venturing onto more populated roadways.
- Teach the necessity of stop, look, listen and think.
- Ride in the same direction as traffic and as close to the curb as possible.
- Never ride a bike across a busy street, always walk.
- Do not ride in wet weather when wet brakes will mean longer stopping distances.
- Never wear long or loose clothes that can get caught in the bike's chain or pedals.
- Never use a personal stereo as the music may hinder the ability to hear traffic.
- Ride in single file and use hand signals.
- Always look right-left-right when entering a road or a crossing as when crossing a street on foot.
- Never ride at dusk or in the evening where possible.
- Ride on cycle paths or lightly travelled streets.
- Teach your child the importance of giving way to traffic and of riding with traffic.
- Look out for cars turning into or reversing out of driveways.

Many local authorities or the community involvement department of your local police station run bicycle-safety classes for children and they are well worth enrolling your child in.

Nine-year-old Kirsten loved the feel of the wind in her hair as she raced along the street on her bicycle. She would imagine herself to be a bird or a bumble bee one day, or an astronaut and airline pilot the next. The faster she pedalled the more exhilarating was the experience.

That afternoon, Kirsten was playing circus acrobats with her friends who were also on their bikes. They would take turns at doing various stunts like riding with no hands or with their feet on the handlebars.

When it was Kirsten's turn, she pedalled really hard to build up speed and just as she was about to climb on to her seat and up into a standing position, her foot slipped from the pedal and jammed itself against the bike's metal frame.

Kirsten screamed with the pain but managed to keep control of the bike until it stopped. Her friends helped her to the side of the road while one of them ran for help. Kirsten's dad tried to free his daughter's ankle, but her screams of pain forced him to call out the fire brigade. It took them 40 minutes to free Kirsten's foot.

Once free, Kirsten was taken to the local hospital where the cuts, bruising and swelling were treated.

Kirsten was lucky.

*   *   *

Nine-year-old Jason was on his way to a local football pitch where his friends were waiting for him before a game of footie. As Jason pedalled furiously along a line of parked cars, the driver of one of the cars suddenly opened a door right in Jason's path. The impact threw Jason head first over the handlebars and he smashed into the solid car door. He was killed instantly.

* * *

In another incident, eight-year-old Susannah was coasting down a long hill near her home when the strap of her school satchel snagged in the spokes of the bicycle's rear wheel. Her neck snapped when she hit the ground after being hurtled over the handlebars.

* * *

Five-year-old Edward was eager to see his best friend's new puppy and was practically standing up as he vigorously pumped the pedals. He either didn't see the pothole in the road, or didn't know that hitting such a pothole at speed could fatally injure a child his size.

Hospital emergency rooms deal with bicycle accidents every day. The injuries they treat range from cuts and bruises to severe facial and body grazing to broken arms and legs to severe head injury which can result in death.

Keep your child's bike safe to ride

Just as you would regularly make simple maintenance checks with your car, ensure your child's bike is safe to ride by regularly checking for mechanical and structural problems such as:

- Brake failure.
- Wobbling or disengagement of the wheel or steering mechanism.
- Difficulty in shifting gears.
- Chain slippage.
- Pedals – loose or falling off.
- Broken spokes.
- Replace all worn, missing or damaged parts.
- Tighten and adjust loose parts.
- Inflate tyres to recommended pressure and replace worn ones.
- Ensure all moving parts are kept oiled and cleaned being careful not to get oil on the tyres.
- Store bicycles in a dry area as moisture causes rust which damages metal parts.

Helmets

Head injury is the leading cause of death in bicycle crashes. Studies have shown that wearing a bicycle helmet can reduce head injuries by up to 90 per cent. It is estimated that about three-quarters of bicycle-related fatalities among children could be prevented by wearing a helmet. And, as young children suffer a higher proportion of head injuries than older children, parents should ensure that their youngster wears a helmet right from the start, even when pedalling their tricycles. A simple backwards fall from a trike onto a cement patio can cause a young child a nasty injury.

A helmet should have a snug but comfortable fit. It should sit on top of your child's head in a level position, and it should not rock forward and backwards or from side to side. The helmet straps must always be buckled. Parents should not purchase it as something a child will grow into later.

Your child is more likely to keep his cycle helmet on once he is out of your sight if his friends wear one too. If you suspect that one or more of your child's friends do not wear a helmet when cycling, have a word with their parents as well as those whose children do wear helmets. A little group pressure may help save the life of their child as well as yours.

Cycling with your baby
Do not cycle with your baby if he is younger than six months old and always use a child cycle-seat that is sturdy and mounts on the back of your bike.

Make sure your baby always wears a cycle helmet.

IN-LINE SKATES AND OTHER SKATING SPORTS
Skating is not without its share of accident risks which makes it important for parents to take time to teach their child to skate properly and to explain fully what the dangers are and how to prevent them.

Protective gear is another must. Make sure your child wears a helmet, elbow pads, knee pads, wrist guards and gloves.

The following are some safe skating guidelines:
• Ensure your child knows how to stop safely.

- Skate on smooth, paved surfaces without any traffic.
- Avoid skating on streets, driveways or surfaces with water, sand, gravel or dirt.
- Never skate at night. It's hard for others to see your child and equally hard for your child to see any obstacles.
- Never skate in the street.
- Learn how to fall. Falling correctly can often help reduce your child's chances of being seriously injured.
- Teach your child that if he feels himself losing his balance to immediately crouch down so that he will not have to fall as far. In a fall, try to land on the fleshy parts of the body and to roll rather than absorb the force with his arms. Even though this may be difficult, explain to your child to relax during a fall rather than stiffen as this may also help reduce injury.

Ice skating

Like other types of skating, your child should wear proper clothing, in particular heavy trousers and jumpers which will help cushion their falls as well as keeping them warm.

As with many sports, lessons will help teach your child to skate properly thereby reducing the likelihood of accidents. Properly managed ice rinks will hold separate sessions for advanced skaters as well as patrols on the ice making sure fast skaters do not make beginners fall.

HORSE RIDING

Insist that your child always wears a proper riding hat every time he gets on the horse. Make sure the hat is a good fit and that your child knows how to fasten it correctly. He should also have proper footwear and clothing for this sport.

Lessons from a reputable stable are another must as they will ensure the horse suits the rider. They will also teach your child guidelines for taking a horse on to a road.

BABY BUGGIES

Do not use a buggy that does not have a safety strap as many injuries occur when children are not securely strapped in. Check for a wide sturdy base and a locking device to prevent accidental folding. Be sure that your baby's fingers are out of the way when folding or closing the buggy.

One horrendous practice that many parents do when crossing the road is to push their child's buggy out into the road in front of them, then stopping to see if any traffic is coming. If a pedestrian crossing is not available, always cross where you have clear visibility from the kerb side.

Never hang bags of shopping and any other heavy item from the buggy's handles as it may tip it over backwards. Always place items in the basket underneath.

Never tie your dog lead to the buggy. If the dog makes a sudden lunge it will either take the buggy with it or tip it over.

STRANGERS

Do not make it easy for a stranger to attract your child's attention by addressing him by name. Keep your child's identity a secret by making sure his name is on the inside of any items of clothing or a schoolbag. Teach your child to raise attention to himself, yell 'help' and run away if a stranger tries to touch or grab him. Make sure your child knows never to get into a stranger's car or go into a stranger's home.

SAFE SHOPPING
When you take your child shopping always keep him by your side. Do not expect shop staff to look after your child and never use toy or book departments as alternative child-minders.

Never leave your child alone in a shop, a car, a stroller, or any public place, even for a moment. And do not allow your child to enter a public toilet by himself. Always go with him.

Your child should know what to do if he gets separated from you while you are out. Make a habit of pointing out shop assistants and reminding your child that should he get lost and cannot find you he should always go directly to a shop assistant and ask him or her to find you. Stress to your child that he should never leave the shop.

ADVICE FOR A CHILD ON HIS OWN
Walk through your neighbourhood, or any areas that your child may frequent without you, to identify problem areas. Point out places to stay away from such as vacant houses (dangerous people may use them), a street or lane with poor lighting, waste ground or play parks that might be a hangout for unsavoury characters, construction sites, ditches, canals, rivers or any body of water.

Then clearly explain the safest routes for your child to take while going to school, a friend's house, the shops or the park.

Your child should always use the 'buddy system'. It is much safer to walk in groups than alone.

It pays to know the names of your child's friends, where they live and their telephone numbers. Always know when your child is going out without you and where he is going. Ask how he will get there, who he will be going with, when he will be back, and of course the address and telephone number of the place where he will be.

Be interested and involved with what your child does when you are not around. Know where he is going, his favourite places and know the other adults who are involved.

Your child should know personal safety and the difference between a 'good' touch and a 'bad' one and to always discuss something with you if it has made him uncomfortable

Teach your child how to call you through the operator on reverse charges. Give your child a telephone card.

TEACH YOUR YOUNG CHILD COMMON SENSE

Make a game out of teaching your young child his telephone number and other telephone safety tips. Write your number on a large piece of paper and cut each number out separately, scramble them up so they are out of order and ask your child to put them back in order to form your telephone number.

Turn your address into a rhyme and sing it each morning with your child.

Your child may one day find himself in an emergency situation. By teaching him a number of different scenarios you may save his life or yours. Make a game of 'what if' with your youngster, providing him with a number of different scenarios and discussing how he would handle them. Then ask, 'what if mummy fell and could not get to the telephone?' or other scenarios and let your child tell you how he would respond.

Every young child should be taught how to dial 999. It's a skill that could some day save a life. Though your toddler might not be able to do anything but cry down the telephone, emergency operators can trace the call as soon as the number is dialled. Practise dialling 999 with your child during a game of 'what if' where you play at being the emergency operator.

SAFE CAR SENSE

Every year children are killed or injured because they are not properly restrained while travelling in a car.

In a 30-mph crash, an unrestrained child continues to travel forward at 30 mph toward the front seat or windscreen. A sudden stop or crash will hurl an unrestrained child forward with a force similar to falling from a three-storey building.

An unrestrained adult holding a child on her lap puts the child in a position of being crushed between the adult and the dashboard or front seat.

Many people feel they are strong enough and could brace themselves quickly enough to hold on to their child in case of an accident. By the very nature of accidents, we do not expect them to happen and when they do they happen so quickly that we have very little time to react. So how could a person expect to react so fast that she could brace herself and hold onto a child if the driver could not react fast enough to avoid the accident in the first place?

If you were holding a bag and a car drove by at 40 mph and grabbed your bag, do you think you could hold on to it? Of course not. The same applies to the child in your lap.

Never, ever, share your seat-belt with a child. In the event of an accident or emergency stop, you would literally crush your child with your body weight as it slams forward into the seat-belt. The safety-belt is designed for single person use only.

Though many parents want to put their new babies in the front seat where its easier to see them, it is safer for your child to travel in the back.

Parents with children who require constant attention should avoid travelling alone where possible. There is an increased risk of crashing which is caused by distraction if the driver is having to constantly pay attention to the child.

Try to keep a child from getting bored on journeys by providing him with plenty of toys or books, if travel sickness is not a problem. Games of 'I-spy' will also help take a child's mind off the miles. Leave plenty of time for the journey and plan plenty of stops for refreshments, a run around and the toilet. Even choosing a scenic route may help alleviate boredom.

Never leave your child alone in a car. Playful youngsters can easily release the handbrake, mess around with cigarette lighters or open the door in the path of oncoming traffic.

If your child is to be left alone in the car for a short time, such as when you fill up with petrol, he should always be restrained and the child-proof locks engaged.

Never allow your child to travel in the boot space of an estate car or a hatchback unless proper seats with restraints are fitted.

CHILD SEATS

The safest place for your child to travel is in the back seat of the car with a proper child-seat according to your child's age or weight. Ensure the restraint is tightly secured and that it does not move excessively when pushed or shaken. An infant might need extra head support and many child seat manufacturers make these head supports for their infant seats. But if you cannot get one, rolled towels round the sides of the head will give extra support.

Rear-facing child seats are generally for babies up to about nine months of age. Your child will then move on to a forward-facing seat. These can provide excellent protection when they are used properly and should be placed in the back seat rather than the front. Remember that not all car seats fit all makes of car. When buying your child seat, have the shop's staff show you how to fit it in to your car and check it for a proper fit. A seat that wobbles excessively will not offer the same protection to your child as a seat that fits snugly. The seat should not move more than two inches forward and back or side-to-side, when it is in place.

Once your child seat is secured, adjust its harness every time it is used to take account of what your child is wearing. There should be firm pressure between the seat-harness and the child.

By the time your child reaches approximately four years of age or 40lbs in weight, he is ready to move to a booster-seat. These give the child extra height so they fit into an adult's seat-belt more comfortably and safely. Boosters also help children see out of the windows which is very useful if your child suffers from travel sickness.

Never put a seat-belt's shoulder strap behind a child. Your child's booster seat should let the shoulder strap sit comfortably across your child. The lap-belt is equally important – make sure it's positioned low and snug across your child's hips. Do not let it rise over the abdomen where the belt could seriously injure your child in the event of a sudden stop or accident.

Do not teach your child to free himself from his car seat.

Cover the seat if the car is left in direct sunshine: metal fittings can become very hot.

Replace the seat if there is any sign of fraying in the webbing, or if the car is involved in an accident, even if there is no visible damage to the seat.

Do not buy a second-hand seat unless its history is known and the correct fitting instructions are with it.

AIR BAGS

Air bags are a proven safety success. They have saved thousands from serious injury or death.

Air bags can cause adverse side effects, too. Nearly all are minor injuries like bruises or abrasions and these are more than offset by the lives they save. Some air bag injuries, however, are serious and can kill. They occur when someone gets in the path of an air bag early in its inflation. Because children are lighter than adults, their risk of serious injury is greater. You can eliminate this risk by putting your child in the back seat and use appropriate restraints according to your child's age.

Infants in rear-facing restraints and unbelted children travelling in the front seat with passenger air bags are among those at risk. Never put a baby in a rear-facing child seat in the car's front seat if it has a passenger air bag fitted. It has been known for babies to have their necks broken and died when air bags have inflated.

SHOPPING TROLLEYS

Shopping trolley accidents are rarely talked about but every year children are injured, sometimes quite seriously, from injuries involving shopping trolleys.

Fractured skulls, concussion and other internal injuries are commonly suffered by children when they jump or fall from shopping trolleys or if the trolley overturns or if they get pinched in the folding seat mechanism or they fall against the trolley.

A child that is allowed to roam the supermarket's aisles while you shop is also at risk of being injured from running into or being hit by other shoppers' trolleys; from tipping a trolley over while climbing on to the outside of the basket and from getting fingers and toes caught in the wheels. He is also likely to pick things up on the way and could put them in his mouth and choke.

Falls by unrestrained children from shopping trolley seats and baskets are the most common accidents. Many shopping trolleys have a high centre of gravity and a narrow wheelbase making them top-heavy when loaded and therefore easy to tip over, especially when the child is in the seat. When children stand up their chances of falling or tipping the trolley over increase.

If your trolley has a lap-belt, make sure you securely fasten your child with it. Remember it is there for a reason. Always use safety-belts to restrain your child in shopping trolley seats.

Consider bringing a harness with you when you go shopping to prevent your child from falling or climbing out of the trolley.

Always stay close to your trolley.

Never let a child push or steer the trolley.

SHOPPING CENTRES

While shopping centres have the attraction of being away from cars and roads they are not without their own safety risks.

Never take your baby's buggy on to an escalator. The balancing act you have to do is far too risky.

If taking young children on an escalator, carry them if possible as they can be slow to jump off at the other end and might fall and hurt themselves. They might also cause a pile-up of people from behind.

Watch out for balconies or any railings that your child could climb up on to or any gaps that he might crawl through.

If the centre has a water fountain, make sure you keep a close eye on your child to prevent drowning.

If changing your baby in a mothers' room, keep all nappy-changing supplies close at hand. It is also a good idea to try and keep a firm grip of the child at all times.

In car-parks make sure your child stays close to you and secure the child inside the car before putting away the shopping.

DANGEROUS GAMES

All children should be taught that rough play can sometimes end in tragedy. Throwing stones, golf balls and other missiles is definitely not on, as in the case of 12-year-old Peggy.

> Like her friends, Peggy was desperate for the extra pocket money that could be earned picking potatoes at the nearby farms during the school holidays.

Her parents consented, happy that she was eager to earn some money for herself.

The first couple of days the farmer and his farm hands were nearby making sure the kids knew what they were doing. By the third day the farmer was content to let the kids get on with it, as they appeared to be a sensible bunch and knew what they were doing.

By late afternoon, some of the kids had become bored with the strenuous work that was involved. Somebody lobbed a potato at one of the other pickers. It was done good naturedly and the person threw one back in the same fashion. Some of the other kids then joined in. After a couple of hard hits, the fight was no longer a bit of fun, it was all-out war.

At first, Peggy and her friends had joined in the laughter. But it wasn't at all funny now and they were trying to make an escape. As they tried to make a run for it across the fields Peggy suddenly felt a searing pain in her head. She passed out.

When she came to her friends were screaming at everyone to stop throwing the potatoes and to get help. Peggy had been hit hard by a potato in the eye.

An ambulance took Peggy to hospital where she underwent emergency surgery to save her left eye. Unfortunately the damage was too severe and surgeons were forced to remove it.

Peggy now wears a glass eye in its place.

Hospital emergency rooms see a lot of injuries from kids throwing things at each other which can result in anything from cuts and broken teeth to concussion and fractured skulls. The summer months tend to be the peak time, report hospital staff, particularly for head injuries caused by golf balls and clubs.

SWIMMING

Your local swimming-pool is more than likely the safest place to go, especially as there are trained life guards on hand should anything go wrong.

All children should be taught how to swim and the younger they learn the better.

Like everything else, children have to be taught good pool sense. Children should never run about the sides of the pool or in changing-rooms. Apart from the fact the floor might be slippery and they could fall, they might knock someone else over.

Teach your child not to jump or dive into a pool on top of other swimmers or if other swimmers are very nearby.

And they should be taught never to dive into a shallow pool. A person who dives into a shallow pool risks breaking their neck.

They should not go down a water slide, chute or flume too close to the person in front. Nor should they go down in pairs or more as this could lead to one or all of them being hurt.

Babies love water and it's a good idea to get them used to it from an early age. If you decide to take your baby or toddler swimming make sure the water is warm. Most toddlers' pools have water so warm it's almost like a bath!

Do not keep your child in the water for too long and

make sure their head is always kept above water. Swallowing too much water can be harmful.

Never take a toddler into a pool without his swimming costume on as it will help contain any mess your child might make!

OUTDOOR SWIMMING

Teach your child to stay away from rivers, lakes, canals or disused water-filled quarries or gravel pits. They are dangerous due to their cold, deep waters, strong currents and weeds that can tangle round a child's feet and pull him under.

Beaches are not always a safe place to allow your child to go swimming either. Sharp currents can pull a child out to sea and fast tides can cut you off from the shore.

Playing on rocks also has its risks apart from a child falling and hurting himself. Large waves can suddenly crash over the rocks, knocking a child off his feet onto the rocks or dragging a child out to sea.

It's advisable for your child to wear sandals or soft canvas shoes on the beach to protect feet from shards of glass or used needles. Keep on the lookout for dog mess too.

HOLIDAYS

Whether holidaying in this country or abroad try to stay in hotels or apartments that are suitable for children. Check to see what kind of family rooms they offer, whether a trained nanny runs the children's club and see if the swimming-pool is fenced in.

If you are travelling by ferry keep a close eye on children and do not even allow older children to wander out alone on to decks or gangways.

On planes, trains or at service-station restaurants remember that your excited child is more likely to spill or knock over hot food and beverages that can scald.

Always take the time as soon as you arrive at your destination to carry out safety checks, both inside and outside your accommodation.

If you do not have ground-floor accommodation, be extra vigilant about open windows or balconies. Rearrange furniture if it's under a window to stop your child from climbing out. It might also be a good idea to remove any chairs or tables from the balcony.

Check the gaps between the balcony railings. If they are more than four inches apart or have bars that enable your child to climb up them, then ban your child from the balcony. Keep the door locked at all times and hide the key.

If you have taken your child abroad, remember that in most countries traffic travels on the opposite side of the road and can cause confusion for children, as well as adults, crossing the road.

In self-catering accommodation the same kitchen rules apply that you insist on at home. Make sure that no electrical appliance leads are dangling down, particularly from the kettle and toaster. Go through cupboards and drawers and remove sharp or heavy items and place them out of your child's reach. The same goes for any cleaning products.

Take a lockable vanity case for all medications and toiletries.

Make sure an adult is always with your child at the poolside. Be strict about no running as wet concrete can be very slippery. Young children should always wear armbands or safety vests in the water.

SPECIAL DAYS OUT

Theme parks and fairgrounds are always a big hit with children. But a bit of forethought and planning will help your day out be an enjoyable one.

Do not queue up for a ride only to find that your child does not satisfy the height restrictions. Check the regulations beforehand as it will save a lot of unhappiness and tantrums.

Check that the ride is suitable for your child's age group. It's cruel to take a child on something that will terrify the living daylights out of him.

Keep a wary eye on youngsters to prevent them wandering off and getting lost. It might be a good idea to insist that your child wears a wrist strap with the other end attached to you.

On all rides, make sure your child keeps his hands inside the moving vehicle.

FISHING

Fishing trips must also have a set of ground rules:

- Never let your child go fishing by himself.
- Insist your child always wears a life-jacket if fishing from a boat.
- Teach him to check that no one is in the way before casting his line. Hooks and flies can cause nasty injuries.
- If fishing from rocks, only do so when the water is calm to prevent waves from washing your child away or knocking him off his feet.
- Keep your child away from areas which have crumbling or steep edges such as quarries or steep river banks.
- Always let someone know where you are going and when you will be back and do not deviate from this.

PETTING FARMS AND ZOOS

While the majority of petting farms and zoos are designed to keep children and animals safe there is always the risk of something going wrong.

Do not allow your child to stick his fingers into cages. Many of these animals are used to receiving titbits from visitors and might mistake a finger for a juicy treat.

Animals at petting farms are usually very mild-mannered and are used to having children around them. Teach your child how to properly pet an animal. Never allow it to jab things into the animal's face or eyes as no matter how even-tempered the animal is, it might not tolerate abuse.

Do not allow your child to climb into animal pens. A fully grown sow or cow can do a lot of damage if it treads on a child's toes. A toddler is at risk of drowning if he falls into a water trough.

A close eye should also be kept on small children who might put an animal's dry-feeding pellets in his mouth as they may cause him to choke.

Make sure your child stays off walled enclosures. They are designed to keep animals in, not as a viewing-seat for your child. Serious accidents have occured when parents have allowed their child onto these walls and they have fallen into the enclosures.

BONFIRE NIGHT

The media is full of horror stories every year of children suffering tragic accidents as a result of fireworks or an unsupervised bonfire. Take your child to a properly organised event rather than allowing him and his friends to have one of their own.

Hold small children by the hand throughout these events

and do not let your child run or play near the bonfire.

If you do decide to have a bonfire party in your own garden remember to obey the firework code – a leaflet about which can be obtained from local government offices, the police and the fire brigade.

Build your bonfire away from the house, fences, outbuildings and plants and keep it small. If there's a strong breeze blowing be extra cautious.

Do not use petrol or paraffin to keep the fire burning once it is lit as the flames can leap into the container.

Make sure there is a bucket of water close by in case the flames begin to spread.

Always keep matches out of children's reach.

Only take one firework out of the box at a time and keep the lid closed.

Never throw a firework or keep them in a pocket.

Never go back to a firework that has not gone off.

Sparklers stay hot for a long time after going out, make sure that you have a bucket of water nearby so that used sparklers can be dropped into it and so lessen the chance of your child being burnt.

CHECKLIST

❑ Dress your child in bright clothes while out on his bike.

❑ Ensure your child always wears a helmet and that it fits correctly.

❑ Teach your child traffic rules and common sense cycling tips.

❑ Cycling should be restricted to pavements and paths until the child is able to ride well and demonstrate traffic sense.

❑ Your child's bike should suit his ability.

❑ Spell out the dangers of irresponsible riding.

❑ Keep your child's bike safe to ride by regularly maintaining it.

❑ Make sure your child knows to skate safely.

❑ Make sure your child knows what a stranger is.

❑ Keep your child safe from strangers by setting up ground rules for when your child is by himself.

❑ Every child should know how to dial 999 in an emergency.

❑ Never allow your child to travel in a car unrestrained.

❑ Your child should never be left alone in a car.

❑ Ensure your child seat is safely and correctly positioned.

❑ Never put a child in a rear-facing child seat in the front seat of a car which has a passenger air bag fitted.

❑ For safety, your child should travel in the back of the car.

❑ Young children should be made to sit in a shopping-trolley's seat.

❑ Do not let young children roam supermarket aisles or climb on the outside of a shopping trolley.

❑ Teach you child how to cross the road and discuss other road safety issues frequently.

❑ Make sure your child knows the dangers of swimming in rivers, canals, quarries and lakes – encourage him to use the local pool.

❑ Ensure your child wears proper clothing and protective gear while playing sports.

❑ Beware of hidden dangers at shopping centres – don't assume that because the shops are indoors your child is safe to roam unattended.

❑ Holiday accommodation should be baby-proofed as much as possible. It's also a good idea if you have older children that might go outside on their own to have a walk around the property with them to make sure it's safe to do so.

❑ Special days out are usually successful if parents have properly prepared for the event – e.g. knowing which rides are suitable and carrying a supply of light snacks and drinks.

❑ Everyone will have a good time on Bonfire night if parents are extra vigilant. Brush up on the Firework Safety Code.

CHAPTER TEN

BEDROOMS

If your young child has access to any other bedrooms apart from their own, it is important to make sure they do not come to harm while inside these rooms.

Check frequently to make sure loose coins, jewellery and other small items are not left in reach.

Keep all bedside tables and dressers free from cosmetics, perfume, medications, birth-control pills, alcohol, cigarettes, lighters and ashtrays.

Five-year-old Caroline was playing in her mother's bedroom when she came across a bottle containing an iron supplement. Her pregnant mum called it her 'special baby medicine'. Like all curious children, Caroline wondered what it tasted like. She also wondered if it would make a baby grow in her tummy just like her mum's.

Caroline opened the bottle. It was easy as it didn't have a child-proof lid on it and started to drink some. She spilled some of it on her shirt and on the floor. She knew her mum would be mad if she found that she had made a mess of her clothes so she got some tissues and wiped it off.

Later that evening, her mum found the spilt medicine on the floor. She didn't recall spilling it so she called Caroline into her room and asked if she had touched her special baby medicine. Caroline denied it and then started to cry, a sure sign, her mum knew, that she had.

Caroline's mum didn't think it would do her daughter any harm and put her to bed. But the incident played on her mind all evening and eventually she called the midwife at the local maternity hospital where she was given the supplement. The midwife told her she must take her daughter to hospital immediately as she was in grave danger.

At the hospital, staff there told Susannah that an overdose of iron is as dangerous as an overdose of paracetamol. It, too, damages the liver and affects the blood's ability to clot; without an immediate antidote a person could bleed to death.

Unfortunately for Caroline, it was too late. Her liver had sustained serious damage from which she later died.

Make sure a child cannot climb onto a bed and then climb out of a window or get tangled in curtain or blind cords which could strangle him.

If an older child has bunk beds, take precautions to prevent your child from climbing up. A fall from the top bunk could prove serious. Make sure the gap between the safety railings is narrow and that there is no more than three inches between the top of the mattress and the bottom of the rail.

If your youngster is a fan of jumping on beds, and you allow it, make sure it is always done in the centre of the bed well away from bedside cabinets and under an adult's supervision.

Keep clothes hangers out of a child's reach. Their sharp ends have produced some rather nasty, as well as fatal, injuries.

Children love to look at themselves in mirrors. Mirrored wardrobe doors are a particular attraction and should be coated with a sheet of safety glass.

If the room has a portable television, make sure it sits well back on the table and that its cord is tucked out of a baby's reach.

Sewing kits must also be kept well out of a child's reach.

Check on older kids regularly as they play in their rooms, especially if they have shut the door.

Best friends Fiona and Gregor sat giggling and arguing alternately as they ate their lunch in front of the television in Fiona's kitchen.

Later the pair went upstairs to Fiona's room while her dad read a book in the living-room and her mum, Sally, went into the garden to enjoy the summer sun.

When Sally checked on them an hour later, they were making tents with the duvets from Fiona's and her elder sister's bunk beds. The two eleven-year-olds were having a great time, as they always did when they were together.

A while later Fiona's dad went up the stairs to

tell Gregor it was time he went home for his tea. He poked his head round the door. At first her father thought the pair were playing 'Dead Lions' – a party game in which youngsters pretend to be dead while one child tries to make the others giggle or move.

Gregor looked as if he was standing next to the bunk beds while Fiona lay on the bottom bunk. Fiona's father went over to tickle Gregor, but when he touched the boy he didn't move and that's when he saw the gold scarf. It was wound round both their necks and threaded through a rail on the top bunk.

The father picked Gregor up and struggled to pull the scarf from his neck. He screamed for his wife to come help while his eldest daughter ran to get a knife from the kitchen to cut the pair free. He then lay the pair of them in the recovery position while Sally dialled 999. An ambulance controller instructed Sally how to give the kiss-of-life and heart massage which she shouted to her husband upstairs. Then she too ran upstairs to help.

Despite the couple's best efforts, the children died.

Later, Gregor's sister told the parents that the pair liked to tie each other up, then see who could escape the quickest. Sometimes, she said, they liked to play torture and bound each other by the neck.

DRESSING-UP

Most children love to dress-up in their parents' clothes. For their sake as well as yours, do not allow your child to play with your favourite Armani suit if you will be upset if it gets ruined. Put some old clothes aside specifically for your child to play with and explain that these are the only ones that he can use.

Keep an eye on your child when he is dressing-up, particularly if you let him play with belts, ties or scarves. He is more liable to trip, fall or catch a part of the fabric or item on something which could result in a nasty injury. Do not let your youngster teeter about in your high heels. Little ankles break easily.

EXERCISE EQUIPMENT

Exercise machines are not climbing frames. With their gears, chains and heavy flywheels these machines are dangerous and can quite easily sever a child's little fingers. Put them in a room that is off limits and is locked from the outside. The same rule should apply to other heavy weight-training and exercise equipment.

CHILDREN'S CLOTHING

Remove hood and neck drawstrings from all clothing. In the UK they are outlawed from being incorporated in children's clothing. Throw away any old sewing patterns that include hood or neck drawstrings in their designs. Never allow children to wear necklaces, handbags, scarves or clothing with drawstrings on play equipment. All too often these items get caught on something and strangle a child.

Waist and ankle drawstrings also pose a threat and as a parent you must decide whether you permit your child to wear items of clothing that contain these. Imagine if the drawstring on your child's coat got snagged on a bus handrail or door without the driver realising.

Consider alternative fastenings for your child's clothes such as fasteners, buttons, Velcro or elastic.

CHECKLIST

❑ Bedside tables and dressers should be free of cosmetics, medicines, alcohol, cigarettes, lighters and ashtrays, aftershaves and perfumes.

❑ Are beds away from windows? If not do windows have safety locks and guards fitted?

❑ Are walls, windowsills and woodwork free of flaking paint?

❑ Are curtain and blind cords tied up or cut off?

❑ Are toxic plants kept well out of reach?

❑ Do you always put clothes hangers away as soon as a garment is removed?

❑ Do mirrored wardrobe doors have safety glass?

❑ Is your portable television sited safely with power leads safely tucked away?

❑ Are all pieces of exercise equipment safely stored?

❑ Have you checked your child's clothing for hood and drawstrings?

CHAPTER ELEVEN

FOOD SAFETY

When it comes to a clean kitchen most people think of shiny floors and gleaming worktops. While this is an essential part of it, a truly clean kitchen is one that ensures safe-food practices – in particular food storage, food handling and cooking.

The very young and the very old are particularly vulnerable to food poisoning which can have serious consequences including death.

FOOD HANDLING

Just as insufficient cooking could cause food poisoning so could poor food-handling practices. Very often foods were safe when they were bought or first prepared. Carelessness in handling and preparation, poor hygiene, insufficient cooking or improper cooling and storage can allow bacteria in food to increase to dangerous levels. Food poisoning can also come from cross-contamination. This occurs when bacteria from raw foods such as chicken or beef comes into contact with something that has already been cooked or is ready to eat, such as fruit and vegetables. In order to prevent this, raw meat and pre-cooked meat, such as ham, should be stored on different shelves in the fridge. Ideally, raw meat should be stored in the salad compartment or bottom shelf of your fridge so that any juice from it does not touch other food. Keep all foods in the fridge covered.

Your kitchen should have two chopping-boards – one for raw meat products and one for fruit, vegetables and other foods. Be careful not to mix the two up. If you only have one chopping-board never use it to cut up raw meats and then immediately use it for chopping up vegetables. Give it a good scrub with washing-up liquid and hot water, followed by a clean with an antibacterial kitchen cleaner. Make sure the board is rinsed well if it is to be used immediately. This should prevent any cross-contamination.

Never wipe up spilled meat juices and then continue to wipe up the rest of the kitchen's work surfaces. This will just spread bacteria all over the kitchen.

Do not forget to wash your hands both before and after handling food and especially after handling raw meats.

Do not scratch your head, wipe your nose or lick your fingers while preparing food.

What you do with leftovers is very important to prevent food poisoning. Never leave leftovers to cool at room temperature. Cool the food very quickly – the less time your food is in the danger-zone for bacterial growth the better. If there is a large amount of food left, divide it between smaller pots and then set them, uncovered, in ice-cold water stirring occasionally to quicken the cooling- off process. Remember, life begins at 40°F for most bacteria.

Once bacteria is on the food do not expect a cold fridge or freezer to kill it off: it won't. Only very high and prolonged cooking temperatures will do this. It is easier and safer to cool food quickly and put it in the fridge rather than poison your family by not reheating your leftovers at a correct temperature.

Always wash fruits and vegetables thoroughly under a running cold tap and use a scrubbing-brush.

When serving food, long-handled utensils are best as it reduces the chance of your hands coming into contact with food. Never use your fingers.

Never use the dishes or utensils you used to prepare food in to serve the cooked food.

FOOD STORAGE

Your refrigerator is undoubtedly the food-safety centre of your kitchen. A refrigerator kept at a low temperature will slow down the bacterial growth which can cause food poisoning. Keep a thermometer in the fridge and check it regularly. Refrigerators should be kept at a temperature of 5°C (41°F) or less. At this temperature, the fridge can inhibit the ability of bacteria to spread or produce a poison, but even in the refrigerator, some food mixtures and very perishable foods will still deteriorate quickly.

If you are not going to eat fresh meat, poultry or fish for a few days, put them in the freezer to stop bacteria growth.

Your freezer should be maintained at −18°C (0°F) or less. This will stop bacterial growth but it will not kill all bacteria already present. Its still important to cook food thoroughly.

Put leftovers or prepared foods such as salads in the fridge immediately after cooking or quick-cooling.

Do not keep food if it's been left out for more than two hours. Do not taste it either. Date leftovers so they can be used within a safe time. Generally, leftovers can be safely refrigerated for three to five days. If in doubt, throw it out.

Do not marinade food at room temperature, always cover the bowl and place it in the fridge.

Check your fridge regularly for any foods which are past their sell-by date as they create unpleasant odours as well as contaminating other foods.

Cover all foods before you put them in the refrigerator.

Do not leave any perishable foods out more than two hours. Be particularly careful if taking perishable food on picnics or a barbecue. Transport picnic foods in a properly insulated cool bag with ample frozen icepacks. Wrapping cold foods in newspaper helps keep them cool. Open the cool bag as little as possible and always put the lid back on immediately. If your child takes his lunch to school, use an insulated lunchbox with an icepack if perishable foods are to be eaten. If you do not have a small icepack then a child's juice drink can be frozen and placed in the lunchbox. This will keep the food cool and the drink will have defrosted by lunchtime. Teach him to keep his lunch out of direct sunlight and away from the radiator.

When shopping, buy cold foods last to avoid dangerous levels of bacteria.

Before buying frozen foods make sure they are frozen right through. Refrigerated foods should be cold to the touch. Always check the expiry dates and never buy dented, cracked or bulging tins as these could be harbouring dangerous bacteria.

Keep your fridge clean inside and out. Clean interior surfaces with warm soapy water then rinse and wipe with a mild bleach solution.

COOKING

Keep your family's food safe by cooking it thoroughly according to the recipe or cooking instructions on the packet.

Invest in a good cookery-book that explains what temperatures food should be cooked at and gives hints on good food preparation techniques.

Use a food thermometer if in doubt but, as a general guide, meat should not be pink in the middle; poultry should be cooked until its juices run clear; fish should flake with a fork. Scramble or cook eggs until the yolk and white are not runny.

When reheating leftovers – particularly anything containing meat, poultry or fish – heat the cooking-dish thoroughly at a higher temperature than when it was first cooked. Stir frequently to ensure even cooking. Bring sauces, soups and gravy to the boil.

Take extra care when reheating large quantities of food such as spaghetti or chilli as they do not heat as quickly as smaller batches and bacteria grows quickly when food is between 40°F and 140°F.

DEFROSTING FOOD

Always defrost food in the microwave or refrigerator. Food that is allowed to thaw at room temperature will be growing bacteria on the outer layers before the food has finished defrosting in the middle.

If it is not possible to defrost food in the fridge or microwave, put the frozen food in a water-tight plastic bag and submerge it in cold water. Change the water completely every 30 minutes to ensure the food is kept cold.

When defrosting food in the microwave always follow

the packet's instructions or refer to your oven's operating instructions. Leave about five centimetres (two inches) between the food and the microwave's sides to allow heat to circulate. Small pieces will defrost more evenly than larger pieces of food.

Defrosted foods should be cooked right away.

KEEPING GERMS AT BAY

Keep germs at bay by regularly disinfecting your kitchen. It's not enough to wipe a cloth over the worktops – proper kitchen cleaning solutions should be used.

Pay attention to the cloth or sponge you use too as these can become the most germ-laden item in your kitchen. A cloth that is not regularly and properly disinfected can spread bacteria to other parts of the kitchen and the cooking equipment.

While hot water and washing-up liquid do a good job, bleach and commercial kitchen cleaning products are the most effective at getting rid of bacteria.

Any piece of kitchen equipment that comes into contact with food, such as a chopping-board, should be washed and rinsed then disinfected with a clean cloth and appropriate cleaning product such as one of the many antibacterial sprays on the market.

Do not forget the kitchen sink, as this also needs to be disinfected regularly. Food particles can get trapped in the drain which is an ideal environment for bacterial growth.

Bacteria can also live on hands, kitchen towels, sponges, chopping-boards and knives. Throughout food preparation keep everything clean with hot soapy water and avoid contaminating anything with the juices of raw food. Replace your sponge or cloth every few weeks and use a plastic rather than a wooden chopping-board.

When washing dishes do not allow them to sit in the sink for any length of time as this creates a nasty bacteria soup. It's also best to let your dishes air-dry. Tea-towels used more than once harbour bacteria and should not be used to dry clean dishes.

WASTE DISPOSAL

Proper waste disposal is an important part of keeping your kitchen clean.

Make sure nothing leaks or spills out of your bin – as this will not only create nasty odours but will also attract insects and rodents. A tight-fitting lid is also important.

Clean bins and their surrounding areas weekly with a disinfectant.

E. COLI

Scientists have recently identified a rare but dangerous type of the Escherichia coli bacterium. Most E. coli are harmless, but the E. coli 0157 variant has proved deadly to humans, particularly young children and the elderly. Scientists believe it takes only a small amount of this particular strain to cause illness

In 1996–97, 20 elderly people died in Scotland as a result of a single E. coli poisoning outbreak and hundreds others were ill, some seriously.

E. coli can survive in both the refrigerator and the freezer and can contaminate any food. Undercooked burgers and roast beef, unpasteurised milk, contaminated water and vegetables grown in cow manure have caused illness.

Undercooked mince has been the primary source of the

E. coli 0157 illness as the bacteria can be found on the surface of raw meat which then gets mixed into the rest of the meat during the grinding process.

Thorough cooking kills E. coli 0157. Do not serve beef that is pink in the middle. Proper food handling, such as not allowing raw meat juices to mix with cooked food, will help avoid cross-contamination.

Eggs

Many people are wary about eggs and the risk of salmonella poisoning. Most eggs do not contain salmonella and the risk of contracting salmonellosis from raw or undercooked eggs is extremely small.

Special precautions are needed, however, when eggs are served to people who are particularly vulnerable to salmonella poisoning. High-risk groups are babies and young children, the elderly and pregnant women.

If you are concerned the following guidelines will help reduce the risks:

Avoid raw eggs and foods containing raw eggs such as home-made mayonnaise, hollandaise sauces and home-made ice-cream.

Cook eggs thoroughly until both the yolk and the white are firm. Fried eggs should be cooked on both sides or in a covered pan and scrambled eggs should be cooked until firm throughout.

Lightly cooked foods containing eggs, such as meringues and french toast, may be unsuitable for people in high-risk groups.

Before buying eggs, check that shells are clean and uncracked. At home, store eggs in their original carton and in the refrigerator.

Avoid keeping raw or cooked eggs and dishes that

have egg in them out of the fridge for more than two hours. If you hide hard-boiled eggs for an egg hunt at Easter, either follow the two-hour rule or do not eat the eggs.

COLD STORAGE CHART

PRODUCT	FRIDGE	FREEZER
Eggs		
Fresh in shell use by carton's sell by date	3 weeks	
Raw yolks or whites	2–4 days	1 year
Hardboiled	1 week	
Mayonnaise, commercial (refrigerate on opening)	2 months	
Salads		
Store-prepared or homemade egg, chicken, tuna, ham macaroni salads	3–5 days	
Convenience Foods		
Store-cooked convenience meals (e.g. steak pies)	1–2 days	
Vegetable or meat soups and stews	3–4 days	2–3 months
Pre-stuffed pork or lamb chops, chicken breasts stuffed with dressing	1 day	
Meat		
Mince and stewing meat	1–2 days	3–4 months
Minced turkey, veal, pork, lamb	1–2 days	3–4 months
Hotdogs – opened package	1 week	
Hotdogs – unopened package	2 weeks	
Cold sandwich meats – deli and opened package	3–5 days	1–2 months
Unopened pack of cold sandwich meats	2 weeks	

PRODUCT	**FRIDGE**	**FREEZER**
Bacon	7 days	1 month
Sausages, pork, beef and turkey	1–2 days	1–2 months
Hard sausage sticks, such as pepperoni	2-3 weeks	1-2 months
Ham, cooked whole	7 days	1–2 months
Ham, cooked half	3–5 days	1–2 months
Ham, cooked slices	3–4 days	1–2 days
Beef, steaks	3–5 days	6–12 months
Beef, roast	3–5 days	6–12 months
Lamb chops	3–5 days	6–9 months
Pork roasts	3–5 days	4–6 months
Veal roasts	3–5 days	4–8 months
Tongue, brain kidneys, liver, heart, offal	1–2 days	3–4 months
Cooked meat/meat dishes	3–4 days	2–3 months
Gravy and meat broth	1–2 days	2–3 months
Chicken/turkey, whole	1–2 days	1 year
Chicken/turkey pieces	1–2 days	9 months
Giblets	1–2 days	3–4 months
Chicken, fried	3–4 days	4 months
Cooked poultry dishes	3–4 days	4–6 months
Plain cooked poultry pieces	3–4 days	4 months

PRODUCT	FRIDGE	FREEZER
Poultry pieces covered with broth or gravy	1–2 days	6 months
Chicken nuggets	1–2 days	1–3 months

CHECKLIST

❑ Use a separate chopping board for raw meats, poultry and fish.

❑ Disinfect your kitchen cloth or sponge after cleaning spilt meat juices.

❑ Always wash your hands before and after handling food and do not wipe your nose, scratch your head or lick you fingers while cooking.

❑ Cool and store leftovers quickly.

❑ Wash fruit and vegetables thoroughly.

❑ Serve food with long-handled utensils, not your hands.

❑ Use clean utensils and dishes for serving food.

❑ Keep your fridge temperature at 5°C.

❑ Raw meats, poultry and fish should be double wrapped and stored away from cooked and ready-to-eat foods.

❑ Keep your freezer temperature at –18°C.

❑ Do not eat perishable food if it has been left out of the fridge for more than two hours.

❑ Never marinade food at room temperature.

❑ Clear your fridge of rotting foods.

❑ Keep all foods in the fridge covered.

❑ When shopping buy cold foods last.

❑ Cook food thoroughly.

❑ Always defrost food in the fridge or microwave.

❑ Disinfect your kitchen and kitchen equipment regularly.

❑ Wash dishes quickly and allow to air-dry.

❑ Keep your bin clean and clear up any spills.

CHAPTER TWELVE

ENTRUSTING YOUR CHILD'S CARE TO OTHERS

A child is the most precious gift a person can have. So when you find yourself entrusting his care to someone else it can be quite nerve-wracking.

This chapter offers some guidelines for what to look for in a nursery, a child-minder or an occasional baby-sitter.

NURSERY

Before choosing a nursery, visit a few in your area to see how they operate. Local authorities carry out regular inspections and it might be useful to get a copy of the inspector's report.

Friends, neighbours and relatives could also be useful in recommending a place that their children attend. They have first-hand experience of how a nursery operates, as well as valuable feedback from their children.

Do not be afraid to ask endless questions during your

visits. A reputable nursery should have nothing to hide and would value your interest. Some of the points you might want to raise are:

- What's the ratio of trained staff to children?
- How many children will be in my child's group?
- Are all staff trained in first-aid?
- Do they offer a structured day of activities?
- Is there a safe, enclosed outdoor play area?
- If children are taken out for walks, how many staff are present, and how will they keep older children under control?
- Are both indoor and outdoor toys – such as climbing frames and slides – regularly maintained?
- Is there a kitchen on the premises which can provide my child with a hot meal?
- Is the kitchen kept separately from where the children play?
- Is there a quiet area where young children can sleep?
- What is the nursery's discipline procedure?
- Do they inform parents of all accidents or incidents their child is involved in?
- What is the fire-drill procedure?
- What happens if I am unable to collect my child and I send someone else?
- Does the nursery have a way of identifying other people who may collect your child?
- Are all doors leading outside of the nursery kept secured to prevent children going out unsupervised and stop strangers wandering in?

CHILD-MINDERS

If you choose a child-minder to watch your child while you are at work it is advisable to choose one that is registered with your local authority. Your local social work department (in England the social services department) should be able to provide you with a list.

As with nurseries, it is advisable to visit a number before making your choice.

Always visit a child-minder in their home. Ask to be shown around. Do not assume that simply because a child-minder is registered that their home is as safe as you would like it be. You owe it to your child to be vigorous about the environment in which he will be cared for.

Below is a list of guidelines to take into consideration before employing a child-minder.

- Test a child-minder's views on safety by asking their opinion on a variety of safety matters.
- Ask the child-minder to show you the household's fire-drill procedure.
- Make sure the house has smoke-detectors and ask them to demonstrate that they are in working order.
- Check the child-minder's registration and insurance documents.
- Ask them to show you where they keep poisonous substances and medication.
- Check for basic safety items like socket covers and stair gates.
- Is the garden enclosed? Is the gate kept locked?
- Are garden toys in good condition?
- Are the toys your child will play with inside the house in good condition? Are there toys for older children with loose or small parts mixed in with toys for younger children?

Look around the house for small items that are lying loose. If you do find any and the minder is already watching other young children, it's probably best that you do not employ this person to watch your child, even if they say they will clear them away.

Glass doors and low windows are another safety hazard to a running child or one riding a tricycle or bike. Ask any potential child-minder whether glass doors have safety-film on them. If there isn't, ask if they are prepared to have it put on. Also suggest putting large colourful stickers at eye-level to make the glass more prominent for children with things other than safety on their minds.

Babies can be very squirmy at nappy-changing time. Ask what arrangements your child-minder has for nappy changing. If it's a raised changing table, ask if they would mind changing your baby on the floor.

If your child-minder has a car which will be used to transport your child, make sure that there are adequate child seats and seat-belts and that the car has valid road tax, MOT and insurance certificates.

Are there pets? If so, ask to meet them when your children are present (see Chapter Fourteen).

Enquire about daytime activities for your child. Do they offer any sort of structured day which includes fun as well as educational activities? Some child-minders spend the day taking children around the shops or planting them in front of the television set so that they can get on with their housework. If this is not the kind of care you want, then it pays to find out in advance of employing this person what they are going to offer your child on a daily basis.

BABY-SITTERS

Choosing a baby-sitter can also be fraught. It's best to go for someone you know, or one that has been recommended by a friend or family member. If you choose to advertise for one, always get references and follow them up.

Always leave a contact name and telephone number of where you will be next to the telephone or taped to the wall if your child is in the habit of removing things. It would be a good idea to add the name and telephone number of your GP.

Ensure the baby-sitter knows your home's layout and explain where important items for your child are kept.

Explain your fire-drill procedure, taking care to point out your established emergency exits – including the ladder if an exit via an upstairs window is required. Make a point of telling the baby-sitter not to try to put a fire out. You want your child safely out of the house first and foremost.

If there is an accident you want to be notified right away unless it's a small cut or bruise that can be dealt with easily. If it's a serious accident and you cannot be contacted quickly, make sure your carer knows to call the family doctor or to dial 999.

Do not ask your carer to give your child a bath unless you are confident about their ability to do so. Children and water require an extreme level of caution and supervision.

A child can drown in an inch of water and it typically happens quickly, silently and when a child has been left unattended or during a brief lapse of supervision. If the child is dirty, suggest that your carer washes him down with a sponge and some warm water.

Ask your carer not to smoke in your home.

It might also be better if your carer did not have any friends round while she's watching your child.

Remind your carer to keep all small items and food out of a baby's and young child's reach. Explain that your youngster has a habit of putting everything into his mouth.

Ask your child's carer to keep toys, loose rugs and anything else that looks like it could trip a child up, off the floor and away from glass doors.

Stairs can be dangerous. Remind your baby-sitter to keep stair-gates closed and not to let your child play on the stairs.

Babies can be very squirmy at nappy-changing time. If yours is a real little wriggler, ask your babysitter to change your baby on a changing-mat on the floor. It's also a good idea to have all nappy-changing supplies nearby so the child is not left unattended even for a moment.

Remind your carer that babies in prams, strollers or baby-walkers should never be left unattended – particularly next to stairs or ramps; accidents can happen too quickly and easily and sudden movement could send your child over the edge.

Your child's carer should also keep doors and windows locked at all times. Children have a habit of 'just disappearing' from a watchful eye.

Never open the door to strangers.

> Laura and Jack had recently moved into a new area where they knew few people. As they had two young children spending some time alone together was proving difficult.
>
> Eventually they got to know one of their neighbours, a sweet old lady who volunteered to

watch the children should they ever want to go out.

One Saturday evening they took the woman up on her kind offer. As they were leaving, they told her that the kids were both in bed and that she was to help herself to anything in the kitchen.

The couple were gone just long enough to have a meal at a nearby restaurant. When they returned, the woman was a bit distressed; she was desperate for the toilet, she said, and couldn't find their loo.

The couple thought this was a bit odd but did not say anything. The woman then went on to say what a gem the couple's six-year-old son was and how he showed her where the baby's bedroom was because she couldn't find it when the little girl started to cry.

Finally Laura could contain herself no longer and asked why she had such a problem finding her way about their house.

'I'm registered blind,' the woman explained.

CHECKLIST

❑ Contact local authority for a list of registered nurseries and ask for copies of inspectors' reports.

❑ Chat to friends and relatives about their children's nursery.

❑ Prepare a list of questions and take them with you.

❑ Have a look at the children in the nursery, do they seem happy and content?

❑ Contact social work (social services) for a list of registered child-minders in your area.

❑ Always visit the child-minder in their own home.

❑ Take a list of prepared questions with you.

❑ Ask to see their insurance and registration documents.

❑ If a car is to be used, ask to see valid MOT, tax disc and insurance documents.

❑ Ask for a walk round the house and garden. Specifically ask to be shown what safety devices and precautions they have in place.

❑ If your child has never met your new baby-sitter, introduce them to each other a day or two in advance of the visit.

❑ Show the baby-sitter round the house, pointing out where all the things that they will need are.

❑ Leave contact names and telephone numbers of where you will be.

❑ Ensure they know what to do in the event of a fire.

CHAPTER THIRTEEN

FIRE SAFETY

One of the most tragic facts about children and fire is that they believe they can hide from the flames and be safe. Teaching your child never to hide but to run from fire must be one of the most important duties a parent has towards her child.

Around 100 children die every year in house fires – the biggest single cause of accidental death of children in the home.

Many families die in fires not because of the flames, but because they have been overcome by smoke. So many of these deaths could have been prevented if a smoke-detector had been fitted and properly maintained.

Preparation is the key to fire safety. It is important to be able to spot potential fire hazards and take immediate action to remedy the problem.

SMOKE-DETECTORS

Smoke-detectors save lives. No home should be without one. Your home should have at least one. They are an inexpensive way to save your family's life.

Place a detector next to the kitchen and a separate one next to the bedrooms. It is recommended that at least one detector should be placed on every storey in your home.

Your local fire-safety officer can offer information on how many smoke-detectors you need and where they should be sited.

Check your smoke-detector once a month according to the manufacturer's instructions. It's no good having one if the batteries are flat or the detector mechanism has failed.

Never disconnect a detector. Consider having it relocated rather than disconnected if it is subject to nuisance alarms from cooking.

If it is battery operated, replace them according to manufacturer's instructions.

Excessive dust, grease or other material in the detector may cause it to operate abnormally.

ESCAPE PLAN

Establish a family escape plan in the event of a fire. Make sure your plan includes a meeting place safely outside the house to make sure everyone is out safely.

You should include at least two exits from each part of the house. One should be a door but if it is hot to the touch, it should not be opened. Use your alternative exit which should be a window. Always make sure that keys for window locks are kept handy. If you cannot open the window for some reason, holding a blanket over the pane while smashing the glass will protect you from cutting yourself.

Rehearse your escape plan and routes regularly.

Include small children as a part of the discussion and

rehearsal. It is especially important to make sure they understand that they must escape; they cannot hide from fire under a bed or in a wardrobe. Your life and your family can be saved by foresight, planning, discussion and rehearsal.

If your family finds the only escape is through a first-floor window, and there is not a rope-ladder and there is no time to tie sheets together, hang on to the window's ledge with your feet dangling down before letting go. An adult should go first if there are two of you to catch small children.

Fire-warning devices will give you time to fight a small fire or safely leave your home. Well-maintained equipment will give you the means to fight it. Know how to operate fire extinguishers and keep them handy.

Teach children to raise the alarm by shouting 'Fire!' and then getting themselves out of the house as quickly and safely as possible.

COOKERS

Never place or store pot-holders, plastic utensils, towels and other non-cooking equipment on or near the cooker. These are a real fire-hazard.

Roll up or fasten long, loose sleeves with elastic bands while cooking. Do not reach across a cooker while cooking. Long, loose sleeves are more likely to catch on fire than are short ones and long sleeves are also more liable to catch on pot handles.

Do not place sweets or biscuits in cupboards over the cooker. As mentioned earlier in the book, always place safe snacks in a low cupboard which means your child will be less likely to climb onto worktops or the cooker.

Be vigilant during cooking, especially if using a chip

pan, which is responsible for more home fires than anything else.

CHIP-PAN FIRES

If your chip pan catches fire, switch off the heat source from under it. Never throw water on a chip-pan fire. Cover the pan with a wet tea-towel, a lid or a fire blanket.

If you are unsuccessful at putting the fire out, leave the kitchen – closing the door behind you – and call the fire brigade.

Reduce the risks of fire by drying chips before placing them in the hot fat; never overfill a chip pan with too much oil; don't put chips in a pan that has blue smoke rising from the oil, it will be too hot.

GAS HEATERS AND PORTABLE ELECTRIC HEATERS

Read all operating instructions and adhere to them.

If matches are to be used, light them before turning on the gas supply.

Store all flammable materials and liquids far away from the heater.

Operate the fire at least three feet away from upholstered furniture, curtains, bedding and other combustible materials.

Avoid using extension cords unless absolutely necessary.

If you must use one with your electric heater, keep the cord stretched out and in a place where it's not likely to cause someone to trip or fall over it. Tape it down using proper electrical tape. Do not permit the cord to become buried under carpeting or rugs. Do not place anything on top of the cord.

Never place heaters on cabinets, tables or other furniture.

Never use heaters to dry clothing or shoes.

Protect children by using a fireguard around heaters.

Do not use timer switches to operate your electric heaters.

Cigarettes, lighters and matches
Keep lighters and matches out of sight and out of the reach of children. Children as young as two years old are capable of lighting matches and cigarette lighters.

Never encourage or allow a child to play with a lighter or to think of it as a toy. Do not use it as a source of amusement for a child. Once their curiosity is aroused a child may seek out a lighter and try to light it.

Always check to see that cigarettes are extinguished before emptying ash-trays. Cigarettes that are still burning will light rubbish.

Empty ash-trays before going to bed.

Never leave a lit cigarette or cigar burning unattended in an ash-tray – children love to mimic adults and the result could be fatal.

Furniture
If buying second-hand furniture, check to see that it adheres to adequate fire-safety regulations. Check what to look out for with your local fire brigade or trading standards office. Only buy furniture that carries the fire-resistant furniture label.

Always check furniture where smokers have been sitting.

Smouldering ashes and burning cigarettes can fall

unnoticed behind cushions or under furniture.

Do not leave ash-trays where they can be knocked off or provide a playground for curious young fingers.

MATTRESSES AND BEDDING
Smoking in bed is a major cause of accidental fire deaths in homes.

Place heaters or other heat sources three feet from the bed to prevent the bed catching fire.

FLAMMABLE LIQUIDS
Flammable liquids are a major cause of house fires. Take extra precautions in storing and using flammable liquids such as petrol and paint thinner as they produce an invisible explosive vapour that can be ignited by a small spark, even at considerable distances. Store in child-proof containers with clearly marked labels in a locked garage or shed.

OPEN FIREPLACES
Keep your child safe by fitting a fixed fire-guard to the wall so he cannot pull it over. Never use this to dry your clothes.

Have a sparkguard fitted too to prevent sparks lighting your carpet or rug.

Keep the mantelpiece clear of items that tantalise your child. He will only try and climb up to get them when your back is turned.

CHECKLIST

❑ Replace smoke-detector batteries as instructed.

❑ Clean smoke-detectors regularly with a vacuum cleaner.

❑ Test smoke-detectors monthly.

❑ Do not dry clothes and towels on a heater.

❑ When buying furniture and furnishings, check that the material is fire-resistant or at least low risk.

❑ Chip pans cause fires – use with extreme care.

❑ Put a fireguard in front of an open, electric or gas fire.

❑ Regularly run through a fire drill with your family.

❑ Ban smoking in bed.

❑ Move cooking oil and other combustibles away from the cooker.

❑ Move old newspapers and magazines away from sources of heat.

❑ Check that heaters are positioned away from furnishings.

❑ Find a permanent safe place to keep matches, away from the cooker or your fire.

❑ Call an electrician to check the wiring in your home.

❑ Check for faulty power points.

❑ Check all electrical appliances to see if they need repairing.

❑ Clean the grill and cooker after each use – this makes sure there is no residual fat or grease that could catch fire.

❑ Install a safety circuit-breaker to your fuse box.

❑ Check bins and furniture for smouldering cigarettes before going to bed.

❑ Install fire extinguishers and know how to use them.

❑ Buy at least one fire blanket and know how to use it.

❑ Teach young children never to hide from fires – they must learn to escape.

CHAPTER FOURTEEN

PET SAFETY

DOGS

For generations loving relationships between dogs and children have been depicted in moving tales such as *Lassie*, *Peter Pan* and *Old Yeller*. A dog can be a child's best friend but a dog can also seriously injure or kill a child.

From the time the puppy is brought home, it must be taught not to use its teeth on humans, even in play. Children, or adults, who play roughly or wrestle with a dog encourage it to use its teeth. Dogs equate this kind of play with the kind it employed while a pup in the litter where it was all right to use its teeth. Anyone who has been used to playing with their dog in this manner, pre- or post-baby, should perhaps consider this a game of the past.

As a puppy, your pet needs to be taught to tolerate having its ears, mouth, feet and tail handled, to allow food to be taken from its mouth and its food bowl removed while it is eating. This should be done regularly to make sure the puppy gets used to it. It will also help ensure the puppy is tolerant of children who perform these actions.

Obedience classes are a must for dogs who will spend time with children, just as children must be taught how to behave, respect and play with a dog. Children need to learn that some games are not to be played with dogs and they need to know how to interpret a dog's body language.

If a child tries to pet a dog that does not want to be petted, for some animals their first instinct is to growl. That growl should be enough warning for any child to leave it alone and not to touch it. Dogs raised with proper training and affection would probably just walk away from the child; and this walking away should also serve as a warning to the child. It is important to teach your child when to leave a dog alone as a growl might not be understood by a young child as a warning sign.

Children should also learn how to give their dog commands and enforce them as most dogs, even well-trained ones, do not consider children as figures of authority.

When bringing a puppy to a household for the first time, children should be seated before picking up a squirming puppy as it will usually end up getting dropped.

If you are introducing a new baby to the already present family dog, remember the dog may become jealous just as an older sibling would. Give your dog lots of extra attention and affection, especially in the early days, to prevent hard feelings.

A safe area, such as a dog bed in a quiet part of the house, should be provided for the dog where it can go for a rest. Your child should be taught not to bother the dog when it is in its bed. Over-tired dogs can get cranky too.

Buying a dog for the first time

If you are considering buying a dog for your child consider postponing the purchase, especially if it's a large dog you want, until your child is at least six years old.

Take time when looking for a dog and do your homework. Learn the differences in the various breeds and choose one best suited to your lifestyle and experience. Always buy from a reputable and responsible breeder who puts priority on good temperament and health.

Train your dog properly. Get help if you run into problems. Do not fool yourself into thinking the dog will 'outgrow' it or that the problem will go away on its own.

Teach your children how to behave correctly and safely around animals and to respect them.

If your children are too young to understand, it will be up to you to physically supervise them and protect them from potential harm. Do not take a chance with their safety. If you cannot be there to take care of a problem or if you cannot control your dog or your child – put the dog in a separate area.

Remember that what your dog tolerates from your own children he may not tolerate from someone else's. You need to take extra safety precautions when other children visit and make sure that the children obey your rules.

Never, ever leave a child alone with any dog, no matter how harmless the dog seems.

Food for Thought

A dog's basic temperament, instincts and training have the biggest effects on how the dog behaves and his level of tolerance. Its temperament is inherited, which is why it's always important when choosing a dog to meet both its parents.

A dog will react to situations according to its instincts unless these instincts are constantly worked on through consistent training by its owner. Very few bites happen without provocation, but it is important to remember that provocation can be brought about by what the dog sees as a threat.

Small children should never be left alone with a dog, no matter how trustworthy you feel the dog is. Remember young children do not know when they are in danger. If you have to leave the room, take the child with you or put the dog in the garden or another room.

Teach your child never to run up to a strange dog to pat it. They should always ask the owner's permission first. When patting a dog the child should never reach over the dog's face but approach the dog from the side. Children should never hug a strange dog.

If a dog is visiting a house where it is not used to children, it may become uneasy with their movements and sounds. It's best to put the dog in a safe room where both it and everyone else will feel happier.

Do not try to force your dog to allow a child to pat or play with it.

Statistics show that most dog bites causing serious injury involve medium- to large-sized dogs and children under the age of five. The dog is usually known to the child or is the family's pet.

Five-year-old John was playing in his front garden when the neighbours' dog wandered over. John had played with the golden retriever almost every day for as long as he could remember.

As usual, when the dog came running over, John went to pet him. But on this occasion the dog turned nasty. He lunged at John's face, sinking his teeth into his chubby cheek. As John screamed and pulled away the dog lashed out again, this time clamping John's ear in its jaws.

John's screams and the dog's vicious growling brought his parents and the dog's owners running.

John was taken to hospital where doctors stitched up his mauled face and ear. The dog was destroyed immediately.

Even at such a young age, John knew how to behave around dogs. John's own family had an alsatian and the retriever that attacked him was known to him.

Though many attacks happen from strange dogs, children should never be left unsupervised with dogs, particularly large ones. Even the ones they know.

Even if you do not have a pet dog, your child should be taught how to respect them. Teach your child never to approach a dog by himself and if he becomes frightened of the dog never run away or scream. These actions can result in the dog attacking your child as it may see your child as prey. Once its prey sense is triggered its response is almost impossible to interrupt. The dog is reacting to chemical stimulus, not rational thought, and is extremely difficult to sidetrack.

It is vital to remember that a dog is a dog and a parent can never be 100 per cent sure that it will not bite.

Hygiene
If your child plays in your garden you might want to think twice about allowing your dog to use it as its toilet.

Apart from an aesthetic point, there are health implications for your child who might find your dog's mess an interesting play option.

Roundworm is the most prominent health concern. Roundworm resides in the small intestines of dogs and its eggs are passed to the outside world in the dog's stools. The eggs take two weeks to a month to become infectious so there is little risk from fresh stools. However, the eggs may remain infective in the soil for years which is why it is important to have your dog wormed regularly.

Young children are at greatest risk of exposure. They may inadvertently eat dirt or grass or touch their mouths with hands contaminated with old dog stools containing the roundworm eggs.

If you take your child to play in areas where there is dog mess, keep a careful eye on him and wash his hands immediately afterwards

CATS

Cats can provide a lot of affection and comfort for people, but if you decide to bring one into your own household where young children are present the risks should be considered.

Children may pull a cat's tail, stick objects in its ears, embrace a cat too strongly, poke the cat or anything else that strikes their fancy. To the untutored child this is fun, to the cat it is not. Even the most gentle of cats may respond with a bite or a scratch.

There are many myths about cats, in particular about cats and babies. One is that cats like to suck the breath out of babies; or that cats smother a baby if allowed to sleep in the child's crib. If you already have a cat you will probably realise that these myths are unfounded and good common sense is more than enough to keep both cats and baby safe.

Cats like to snuggle with babies because they are warm, soft and do not make quick movements. You could try letting the cat snuggle with you and the baby while you are nursing or holding the baby. This way the cat will begin to grow accustomed to the sounds, sights and smells of the baby.

When the baby starts to crawl, it will often start reaching for the cat and try and grab hold of the cat's tail or face. At this age the child poses little threat to the cat who can escape if need be.

The toddler stage is a different story. Both the child and the cat will need to be supervised constantly. Even the most gentle of cats may retaliate with a bite or a scratch if your child persists in annoying it.

It is also recommended that kittens are not brought into a household where there are toddlers. Little children with the best of intentions and kindest of hearts can maul a kitten to death. And, kittens' little claws and teeth are as sharp as needles which can inflict a nasty wound to your child.

BUNNIES AND OTHER SMALL, FURRY CREATURES WITH TEETH AND SHARP CLAWS

As with any pet, bunnies, hamsters, gerbils, and guinea pigs need to be treated gently and carefully by your child, especially since these pets are unlikely to respond to obedience classes.

Always provide your pet with a safe place where your child cannot get to it. Take your child's hand and show him how to sit quietly next to the rabbit or guinea pig and pet it gently; or how to hold a hamster, remembering to sit on the floor as the hamster will invariably get dropped from time to time.

If your child does get scratched, use this as an opportunity to explain to your child what he did that made the animal scratch or bite him. Remind your child that rabbits or hamsters are just little and might be scared. This might help prevent any bad feelings the child might have towards his pet if he were scolded and it might prevent mishaps in the future.

If your child has his playmates round, make sure they understand that these little animals can bite and scratch and have to be treated gently and with respect.

Children love pets and with careful adult supervision, patience and guidance your child, too, could develop the same Lassie-type bond which will stay with your child for a lifetime.

CHECKLIST

❑ Teach your child how to play with his pets.

❑ Teach your puppy tolerance.

❑ Take your dog to obedience classes.

❑ Ensure your child knows when to leave an animal alone.

❑ Your child should never approach a strange animal.

❑ Buy your dog from a reputable breeder only.

❑ Never leave a child alone with a pet.

❑ Make sure your child does not torment a pet.

❑ Supervise your child while he plays with pet rabbits and other small animals.

❑ Teach your child good hygiene practices when handling pets.